POETS OF THE DEMOCRACY

ROBERT BURNS.

POETS OF THE DEMOCRACY

BY

G. CURRIE MARTIN

Illustrated with Portraits

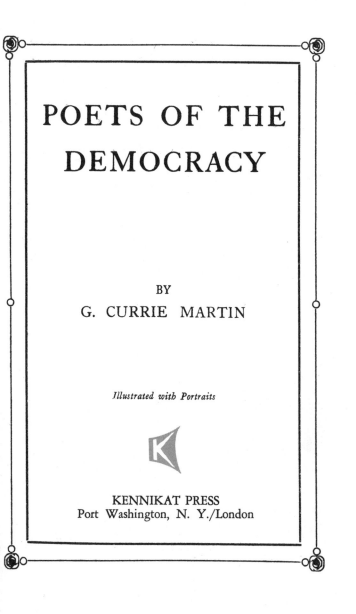

KENNIKAT PRESS
Port Washington, N. Y./London

POETS OF THE DEMOCRACY

First published in 1917
Reissued in 1970 by Kennikat Press
Library of Congress Catalog Card No: 79-11
ISBN 0-8046-1048-7

Manufactured by Taylor Publishing Company   Dallas, Texas

TO THE MEMORY

OF

PROFESSOR DAVID MASSON

IN GRATITUDE

FOR LESSONS LEARNED IN HIS CLASSROOM

ON THE

VALUE OF LITERATURE

PREFACE

*T*HE object of the following pages is threefold. First, to form an introduction to poetry to a large class of readers who have never realised what joy and power lie within that region. It is a sound educational principle to meet one's students along the line of their greatest interest. There are certainly a very large, and it is to be hoped, increasing number of people all over the world, one of whose deepest interests is in democracy. The existing strife in Europe, and the actions of Russia and the United States have exemplified this beyond dispute. By this line many may find an entrance into the realm of poetry, and these sketches may aid them on their journey.

Secondly, these studies are designed to show the readers of poetry how large a place the democratic ideal holds in the poetry of the English-speaking world. It is only that side of their work that can be touched on here in dealing with such masters of the art as *Wordsworth* and *Burns*, and it is to be hoped that this limitation will be recognised by all readers.

Some may he ready to ask why a study of *Shelley* has not been included. The main reason is that his poetry is very difficult, and makes its main appeal to those who love poetry for its own sake, and hence does not find a place in such an introduction to the study as this professes to be. Further, the writer hopes, at some future time, should these papers meet with any measure of approval, to continue the subject in studies of the democratic ideal in poetry that goes beyond the field of writers of *English*. It would then be fitting to show the *Greek* influence on poets like *Shelley* and *Swinburne*, but the background would first require to be examined.

Thirdly, the writer is not without hope that he may accomplish something in spreading a true view of and enthusiasm for democracy by this little book. It is the suprême unifying factor in the present crisis, and all nations will be more ready to listen to its message than they have been formerly. If in any way the study of these pages, and of the poets to whom they point, can further this great cause of liberty he will be more than content.

Already he has received his reward in some measure. Many of the following studies have already appeared in the pages of a magazine, and he has received many messages from the trenches telling him of the help and inspiration they have proved to our men in the midst of the struggle. He hopes that the book may be far more widely useful, and that it may brighten many weary hours.

For permission to republish much of this material in its present form he offers his grateful thanks to the Editor and proprietors of " One and All," in the pages of which the majority of the chapters have already appeared.

Many friends have aided the author by suggestion and criticism, and to all of these he expresses his deep gratitude.

Vailima,
   June, 1917.

CONTENTS

PORTRAITS

CHAPTER I THE DEMOCRATIC IDEAL IN POETRY.

DEMOCRACY has been described as "a spirit and an atmosphere," its essence as "trust in the moral instincts of the people." "No form of government is so feeble as a democracy without faith. But a democracy armed with faith is not merely strong : it is invincible ; for its cause will live on, in defeat and disaster, in the breast of every one of its citizens."* And the prophets of a democracy's faith are frequently its poets. This has been notably so in Italy, where the populace were moved to action in the present struggle against Austria by the words of a poet, and many centuries earlier it was Dante, who not only moulded Italy's language by glorifying the speech of the common people, but made it the vehicle of the finest thoughts of his day on political and religious liberty. Some of our own poets caught the fervour from the same source, and in the verses of Mrs. Browning and Mrs. Hamilton King, the splendid enthusiasms that moulded United Italy touched the soul of our own people. Who that has read them can ever forget the opening lines of Mrs. Browning's *Casa Guidi Windows* with its thrill for liberty so wonderfully expressed ?

> " I heard last night a little child go singing
> Neath Casa Guidi windows, by the church,
> *O bella libertà, O bella !* "

---

* A. E. Zimmern in *War and Democracy,* pp. 1 and 2.

and again,

> " Heroic daring is the true success,
>   The eucharistic bread requires no leaven,
> And though your ends were hopeless, we should bless
>   Your cause as holy. Strive, and having striven,
> Take, for God's recompense, that righteousness."

In the pages of Mrs. Hamilton King's poem *The Disciples*, the same note is struck again and again, and we feel the very soul of the Italian people pulsing in the lines :

> " But higher than the note of trumpet swelled
>   The heart of Italy ; and faster beat
>   The heart of Italy than all the bells
>   That pealed on one another through the air."

In this sense of the term we have a great amount of democratic poetry in English, for the spirit of our people has always been in sympathy with freedom. The following pages will afford many examples, for it is the thread upon which all these studies are strung. In Whitman and Carpenter we find Democracy raised to an even higher pitch, for their verses turn democracy into humanity, and its highest ideals become the ideals of the race, which is indeed the ultimate truth. Carpenter expresses this perfectly in such lines as these :

> " As it ever was and will be—
>   As a thief in the night, silently and where you least expect,
> Unlearned perhaps, without words, without arguments, without
>   influential friends or money—leaning on himself alone—
> Without accomplishments and graces, without any liniments for your
>   old doubts, or recipes for constructing new theological or
>   philosophical systems—

With just the whole look of Himself in His eyes—
The Son of Man shall—yes, shall—appear in your midst.   O beating
    heart, your lover and your judge shall appear.

*   *   *   *   *   *

The Son of Man—
Ponder well these words.
After all, I cannot explain them : it is impossible to explain that
    which is itself initial and elementary,
You will look a thousand times before you see that which you are
    looking for—it is so simple—
No science, O beating heart, nor theology, nor rappings, nor phil-
    anthropy, nor high acrobatic philosophy,
But the Son—and so equally the Daughter—of Man."*

The very title of his book, *Towards Democracy*, suggests his ideal. We have not yet seen Democracy as it is designed to appear in the world. God has once set it before us in the Person of the Son of Man, and when His ideas become universal practice then shall we know. Then shall we have " the new heaven and the new earth wherein dwelleth righteousness." Thus it is that our study of these poets is not only a literary joy, but a religious task.

The democratic idea universalises all this poetry. It is not so much the expression of a race or a single people as the voice of humanity that we feel in these messages. The proof of this is twofold, first that we find in the men we shall study representatives of the whole English-speaking world—including India ; and, secondly, that some of these poets, though not our most famous writers, have drawn their best students and

---

* *Towards Democracy*, p. 51, § xxxv.

interpreters from men of other races than our own. To France, especially are we indebted for some of the most illuminating interpretations we have of their message. Burns speaks to humanity, not to Scotland only, and Whitman stirs kindred emotions in Russia as surely as in the United States.

Nor does this prevent its being true that very often the most democratic voices reach us through the medium of dialect. Dialect is, after all, nothing more than the nature speech of the people. A man always reveals himself most perfectly in the speech of his childhood. Round the words his mother used the tenderest of associations cluster, and through these he can most effectively utter messages that are universal in their import, for thus he can touch the heart of humanity most perfectly. Many of these poets are like David in Saul's armour when they essay another tongue. This is notably the case with Burns, whose English verse never equals the exquisite beauty of his Scots. In order to study adequately poets of democracy we should have to study dialect poetry much more thoroughly than has been possible for our present purposes. The expression is most universal, but the apprehension is more limited. The man can utter himself best in that medium, but his reader is not so much at home, for he lacks the association and atmosphere. To a Yorkshireman poetry in his own speech has a closer appeal than has finer verse in standard English.* The non-Yorkshire man reads them with difficulty and, unless he has at least resided in that county for some time, misses their flavour. Yet no one can truly reach the heart of the Yorkshireman till he knows his language. Thus arises the paradox that the more limited the form of speech the more intense is the appeal, since to the human mind early association is so strong. The thought is reflected and the contention illustrated in the following verse from William Barnes, the Dorsetshire poet :—

> " My hwome were on the timber'd ground
> O' Duncombe, wi' the hills a-bound,
> Where vew from other pearts did come,
> An' vew did travel vur from hwome,
> An' small the worold I did know ;
> But then, what had it to bestow
> But Fanny Deane so good an' feair ?
> 'Twere wide enough if she were there."

Lowell can give us the heart of the American best when he writes in the dialect of the Biglow Papers, and Kipling's appeal to the common man is largely because he speaks his speech. As Professor Dowden† puts it, aristocratic art strives after selectness and is exclusive. By it " directness and vividness are sacrificed to propriety," while to a poet like Whitman " every

---

* See Professor Moorman's volume of poems in the Yorkshire dialect. Leeds. 1s.

† E. Dowden. " The Poetry of Democracy," *Studies in Literature.*

man is a divine miracle." For him " the powerful
uneducated person" is a delight, and to
endeavour to capture and reproduce his point of
view is a great part of his purpose. " In the grass
he beholds the democracy of the fields, earth-born,
with close and copious companionship of blades,
each blade like every other, and equal to every
other, spreading in all directions with lusty life
blown upon by the open air, ' coarse, scented,
fresh, nutritious.' "

One of the most recent poems in the English
language has been inspired by similar ideas,
and the writer has endeavoured to reinterpret
for us the life of the toiler through our centuries
of history. Mr. Maurice Hewlett, in his *Songs
of the Plow*, has made this attempt. We need not
hold that he has been successful in order to
recognise the merit of the effort, and the significance of the choice. Never before has the
attempt been made, and it is easy to criticise ad-
versely a fresh venture. The author is too much
of an outsider to understand fully the men and
women of whom he writes, but he has sympathy
and, like J. R. Green, recognises that the history
of England is not one of kings and battles, but
of the sufferings, hardships, and steady attain-
ments of the people. This morning picture is
very beautiful :—

> "He hears the great slow oxen splash
>   Their way through puddles in the lane,
> The wet wind whistles in the sash
>   Or spatters hasty on the pane—

A hopeless dawn !   Nay, in the West,
  Beyond the fringes of the rain,
See, like an opening palimpsest,*
  Watchful and steadfast, Heaven's blue eye ! ''

Or once more we recognise simplicity of thought
and form in the lines :

" He holds it fast the dawning sense
    That there's a God of simple folk,
  A woman for his reverence,
    A child she rears to bear a yoke."

The great democratic poets have written in
order to bring in a day in which the child shall
not be born to bear a yoke, but enter into a large
and free liberty, wherein there shall be no arti-
fical fetters fastened to their limbs even in their
cradles. They have been the heralds of the
dawn, but they have been more than harbingers,
they have been co-operators. They have
inspired men with a new courage to fight for
fresh conditions wherein life shall be more full of
riches and opportunity. They stand for the
spiritual values, and to read their pages means
for us a further advance in liberty. We cannot
live without them, if our life is to mean all it may
for us and our children. To know them is in
itself a liberal education, and to help in forwarding
this knowledge these studies have been penned.
The more that the spirit of such poetry enters
into the life of the great nations the more
certainly shall we be delivered from all existing
enthralments, we shall recognise that not the

* A manuscript with one writing on the top of another.

least of our deliverers have been the men who have sung of freedom as one of the greatest of the Sons of God.*

The Hebrew poet heard their anthem at the birth of the world and surely among the most joyous of the singers were those named Liberty, Love, Beauty, Joy, Knowledge and Faith.

---

* Job xxvii. 7.

"When the morning stars sang together,
And all the sons of God shouted for joy."

CHAPTER II—
PIERS THE PLOWMAN

IT will be the effort of this series of papers to show how the democratic spirit has from time to time throughout the story of our poetry been revealed and fostered by some of the greatest writers of our land, and how our singers have awakened and expressed the deepest longings of our race.

It is surely not without special significance that the fount of our English song sprang up in the heart of a simple working man—Caedmon, the servant of the Whitby monastery in the seventh century, and the lonely cross erected to his memory many of us know, as it stands facing the sea by the old Abbey on the Yorkshire cliffs. Six centuries later was born the poet of whom we have here to tell. William Langland was a country man, brought up somewhere among the Malvern Hills, the vision of whose beauty never faded from his eyes among the bustle of London streets, in which city he seems to have spent the greater part of his life.

He was probably born somewhere early in the thirties of the fourteenth century and lived till he was about seventy, dying probably in the same year as Chaucer, that is, the first year of the fifteenth century. We know that he had a wife and only daughter, and that he was a tall man who found it hard to stoop in order to enter lowly doors, and went by the nickname of Long Will. His life seems to have been one long struggle against great poverty, his poorly-paid profession being that of a singer of psalms for the souls of the dead. His sympathies were always with the poor among his people, and his heart was torn at the spectacle of their suffering. He saw much sorrow, for he tells us the story of the great pestilences that swept across the land in 1348 and 1361, and the great tempest of January 15th, 1362. Like many a man before and since he saw in these events the hand of the Divine Judge, dealing with the sins of the people.

> " He proved that the pestilences were purely for sin,
> And the south-west wind, on Saturday at even,
> Was plainly for our pride, and for no point else.
> Pear-trees and plum-trees were puffed to the earth
> For example to sinners, to serve God better.
> Beeches and broad oaks were blown to the ground,
> Turning upwards their tails as a token of dread
> That deadly sin, at doomsday, would condemn us all."

This first extract from his poem serves to show us its form, which is so different from our present-day verse, though moderns like Whitman and Edward Carpenter remind us of the manner. It is not rhymed, nor are the numbers of the syllables the same in each line. The principle is that of *alliteration* (*i.e.*, certain syllables in each line beginning with the same letter), and of accent—the voice stress falling, as in a chant, on certain places in the line. Again, each line has a pause near the middle, and *generally* two of the syllables beginning with the same letter come before, and one after the pause.

The poem consists of a series of visions and has often been compared to the *Pilgrim's Progress*. It has no such clear and interesting story as that work possesses, and is indeed rather confused and perplexing in outline, probably owing to the various altered forms in which the poem appeared. Many of the characters are simply moral virtues and vices dressed up as real beings, *e.g.*, Reason, Conscience, Bribery, Falsehood, Flattery, Wisdom, and Wit. Sometimes his invented names are much more cumbrous than those of the latter Puritans, as when he introduces us to Tom-true-tongue-tell-me-no-tales-nor-lying-stories-to-laugh-at-for-I-loved-them-never, or Dame-work-when-time-is. Sometimes place-names are of the same character, reminding us again of Bunyan's topography, as in the lines :

> " Bend forth by a brook named Be-courtly-of-speech,
>   Till ye find there a ford, called Honour-your-fathers."

The vision begins with a field full of folk, who are situated between Heaven and Hell. The way to the former is the way of Love, but there are many pitfalls and false guides. Dangerous among the latter is the lady named Bribery, who is about to be married to Falsehood. The wedding is objected to, and the case has to go to the king at Westminster. The king suggests she should marry Conscience, but the latter indignantly refuses.

Other troubles arise, and eventually the king agrees to have Reason as his constant counsellor.

Then we have a vision of the seven deadly sins, and a pilgrimage in search for Truth. No one knows the way thither, till Piers the Plowman arrives, and volunteers to lead the seekers to their goal. He turns all to work, and the shirkers are driven to obedience by hunger. A violent dispute with a priest who challenges the credentials of Piers brings the poem proper to an end.

A long, elaborate, subordinate poem is often regarded as part of the same work, but is really quite separate. In it Piers the Plowman is a thinly-disguised figure of Jesus, but its story is much too complicated even to outline.

There are many interesting pictures of the life of the people, their food and their work. Luxuries were pullets, bacon, geese and eggs. These the poor man's larder did not know, and Piers gives us his fare as follows :—

> " Some curds and some cream, and an oaten cake,
>   Two bean loaves with bran, just baked for my children.
>
> *   *   *   *   *   *
>
>   Then all the poor people their pea-shells brought,
>   Beans and baked apples they brought in their laps,
>   Young onions and chervils, and ripe cherries many."

Severe satires on contemporary manners and morals crowd the pages. One tells how, as a draper's apprentice, he had been taught :

> " To stretch on the stuff, till it looked the longer,"

and put the cloth in a press

> " Till ten yards or twelve were turned to thirteen."

He is asked :

> " ' Hast thou pity on poor men, persuaded to borrow ? '
> ' Such pity on poor men, as a pedlar on cats :
> Could he catch them, he'd kill them ; he covets their skins.' "

Sloth tells how " his serving man's salary is sometimes behind," and how

> " With wrath and ill-will all my workmen I pay."

There is a wonderful tavern picture, showing how, then as now, so many workmen were deluded by it, and wasted money in drink and gaming. The author has no mercy for laziness in any form, and pours out the vials of his wrath on the ranks of careless church priests who make a hypocritical show of piety. But beggars and beadmen are also profitless bustlers,

> " Their bags and their bellies with bread were well cramm'd,
> By falsehood they fed them, and fought o'er their ale."

In contrast with all such are the hard-working populace—the rank and file of the agricultural labourers.

> " Some ploughed with the plough ; their play was but seldom,
> Some sowing, some earning, with sweat of their brows,
> The gain which the great ones in gluttony waste."

There is for the rich and the oppressors no help unless their lives are altered :

> " Save Do-well you help,
> Your patents and pardons a pea-shell are worth ! "

At the opposite pole to all these is Piers himself, who is the servant of Truth, and the follower of the lowly Master. In the regular routine of daily toil he finds his way of obedience and of service.

> " I have faithfully followed Him fifty long years,
> Both sown Him His seed and His cattle preserved,
> Within and without have I watched o'er His profit,
> I dike and I delve, and do that He biddeth.
> Sometimes I sow, and sometimes I thrash,
> I am tailor or tinker, as Truth doth appoint,
> I weave or I wind, doing whatso He biddeth."

Thus the poem shows to us the way of deliverance for the rank and file of the people, as the author conceived it. The message of the Gospel is the people's charter, and they can find the true path if they will seek it, " under the sole guidance of Reason, Conscience, and of the grace of God." He was not himself a political revolutionary, but he sowed the seeds, which soon in other hands raised the harvest of rebellion. The peasants under such leaders as John Balle and Wat Tyler, found much in his words which justified their action. He was the friend of the poor, for thus he felt himself to be most in accord with the mind of Christ. As he says :

> " Why I move this matter is mostly for the poor,
> For in their likeness our Lord hath oft been known."

We find it difficult to believe that the words he writes are five hundred years old—so appropriate do they seem to many of our own conditions ; and his solution of the problems of his day remains still the only satisfactory one—that all classes should translate into daily action the laws of Christ.

[Note.—The language of the poem is difficult, and might be unintelligible to many readers. The version in modernised English by Prof. Skeat in the King's Classics at 1s. 6d., from which the above quotations are taken, is a most useful edition. So also is that published in Everyman's Library, also modernised. Very interesting will also be found the historical novel entitled *Long Will*, by Florence Converse, in Everyman's Library, 1s., in which the ife and surroundings of the poet are well described.]

CHAPTER III—
FROM LANGLAND TO GRAY.

IN the poetry of William Langland, as Professor Mackail reminds us : " The claims of labour are becoming identified with the claims of life.

> " ' Joy, that never joy had, of rightful judge he asketh.' "

The right to have joy is indefeasible, unless life is to be, in the proper sense of the word, hell. Either here or elsewhere it must be, but the claim is now definitely made that it shall be here, and not elsewhere :

> " ' For all are we Christ's creatures and of his coffers rich,
> And brethren as of one blood, as well beggars as earls.' "

To ' have ruth of the poor ' has become the first and great commandment." It is noteworthy that in Langland's great contemporary Chaucer —a far greater poet—it is just this touch we miss. " In that part of life left out," to quote Professor Mackail again, " there lay, as in the unexplained errors in the calculations of astronomy, the promise and potency of fresh advances among unimagined worlds."

It was a very long time before the note was again sounded—not, as we shall find, till the eighteenth century, and till the dawn of our modern civilisation.

Poets for many centuries took their inspiration from other sources, or, if they dealt with the common people, either slighted them, or described

JOHN MILTON.

them in an unreal world, as in the Arcadia of their fanciful shepherds and shepherdesses.

Even Shakespeare in his greatness had little of the true democratic spirit. He shows us many features of the common people, but it is mainly that we may laugh at their conceit, ignorance or rough horse-play. Now and again we come on a passage that rings with true democratic feeling, as in the speech of Cassius in *Julius Cæsar* :

> " Men at some time are masters of their fates ;
> The fault, dear Brutus, is not in our stars,
> But in ourselves, that we are underlings."

Yet we remember that, in the same play, Antony plays on the mob as on an instrument and befools them to his heart's content. It is the weak, not the strong side of the people, that is most in evidence.

Milton, England's next greatest poet, has not much in his verse that touches the democracy. A line or two in a sonnet breathes the real spirit, and rings in our ears to-day like a trumpet-call.

> " O yet a nobler task awaits thy hand
> (For what can war but endless war still breed ?)
> Till truth and right from violence be freed,
> And public faith cleared from the shameful brand
> Of public fraud."

In another, in which he refers to having lost his eyesight, and puts the question,

> " What supports me, dost thou ask ?
> The conscience, friend, to have lost them overplied
> In Liberty's defence, my noble task,"

In his prose writings Milton shows himself a real democrat, but we cannot touch them here. Once, however, he quotes an old Greek poet, and his own rendering of the lines is worth repeating :

> " This is true liberty, when freeborn men,
> Having to advise the public, may speak free ;
> Which he who can and will deserves high praise :
> Who neither can nor will may hold his peace."

There was a much less known contemporary of Milton, George Wither, on one of whose books we may well linger for a few moments. It is a unique book. There is nothing like it in all the range of our literature, and it is an effort to call the democracy—the whole people from king to peasant—to a better and nobler frame of mind. The volume is known by the quaint title of " Hallelujah, or Britain's Second Remembrancer." The *first*-remembrancer was an earlier volume of Psalms and Hymns. That which now claims our attention was published in 1641, and consists of three divisions comprising what he terms " occasional, temporary, and personal " hymns. It is the last class which most interests us, and in his preface to the section he writes :—" I conceived it a good means to insinuate into persons of every calling and degree, some of these musings and considerations, which are necessary to be remembered." He is very catholic in his range, for his hymns include those for a magistrate, a member of Parliament, a servant, a lover in general, a lawyer, a soldier, a seaman, a labourer, a handicrafts man, a tailor, a jailor, and an innkeeper ! Let us see how he treats some of these themes. Here is part of his counsel to M.P.'s :—

> " Imprudent legislators may
>   Much greater mischief cause,
> And innocency more betray
>   Than they that break the laws ;
> For he that many laws doth break
>   May wrong but one or two,
> But they which one bad law shall make,
>   Whole kingdoms may undo."

The physician is led to pray :—

> " Let the grievance of the poor
>   Be, for charity of me,
> As much tender'd evermore
>   As the rich man's for a fee ;
> And in me their mind prevent
>   Who prolong an easy cure,
> And their profits to augment,
>   Make men grieved more grief endure."

The musician is reminded :

> " He sings and plays
>   The songs which best Thou lovest,
> Who does and says
>   The things which Thou approvest."

To craftsmen he writes :—" All handicrafts being gifts of the Holy Ghost, it were fit men did better know it, and more often praise Him for it ; to that end this Hymn was devised."

> " Embroidery Thy invention was,
>   Though many think it vain.
> The skill to frame in steel and brass
>   We did from Thee obtain ;

> For not Bezaleel's hands alone
>   Didst Thou with cunning fill,
> But yet instructest every one
>   That is endowed with skill.''

Nowhere is he more tender or quaint than in his hymn for an innkeeper, and with a quotation from it we must close for the present the pages of this fascinating book :—

> '' Yea, though our calling many scorn,
>   And brand it with disgrace,
> Our Saviour in a hostry born,
>   Hath sanctified the place.
>
> *   *   *   *   *
>
> So at mine inn Thy blessèd Son
>   His lodging, Lord ! shall take ;
> And there, much more than I have done,
>   Him welcome will I make ;
> For not a stable but my breast
>   Shall be his lodging room ;
> And mine own heart, to give Him rest,
>   A pallet shall become.''

During these centuries it was mainly in anonymous poetry that the spirit and mind of the democracy were most revealed. The songs and ballads are the verses which spring from the common heart of the people, and there we must look for the link that knits the rugged lines of Langland to the poetry that will later claim our attention. It is natural that we should turn back in these days with gladness to the Folk Song of old England as a living expression of our own emotions, for therein the heart of the people is revealed, and our collectors are doing us a great service, as Grundtvig did for Denmark, in bringing to light these long-hidden treasures of

England's best traditions. The songs of different shires knit us together in the common consciousness of needs, moods, and emotions that make us one. The wandering minstrels were the means whereby these songs became widely known among all classes, and they were " equally at home in ale-house, in hall, in market-place, or in cloister, and could sing with equal spirit a ribald and saucy love-song, a convivial glee, a Christmas carol, a hymn to the Virgin, or a doleful lay on the instability of life or the fickleness of riches." These songs had generally a chorus, and it was as popular as it is to-day for the folk to join in the refrain. One of the effects of the war is to revive the love of popular songs, and in our various circles we have no slight duty to foster and cultivate this art, as the splendid new Fellowship Song Book helps us to do.* The songs were love songs, hunting songs, May-morn songs, satires, lullabies and carols in the main. There are yet great stores unexplored, and still more unfamiliar, and we may hope that ere long they will be within reach of us all, for there is much radiance of joy and exquisite beauty of feeling in these verses. One student of the subject writes, " Every wisp of a spring poem has the odour of green things about it, this contagion of happy *abandon*. One little song has only this to say :

---

* *The Fellowship Song Book*, edited by Dr. H. Walford Davies, Headley Bros.

> " ' Trolly, lolly, loly, lo,
>   Syng troly, loly, lo.
>   My love is to the green wood gone,
>   Now after will I go.
>   Syng troly, loly, lo, ly, lo.

Yet how completely it expresses the mood ! "

We have also the ballads, those wonderfully simple and touching narrative poems, many of which come from a remote period, and link together the nations not of Europe only, but of the world. Truly has it been said of them that " they speak not only in the language of tradition, but also with the voice of the multitude : there is nothing subtle in their working, and they appeal to things as they are. . . . They can tell a good tale. They are fresh with the open air, wind and sunshine play through them." They are far too long to quote, for a verse or two gives no idea of them. If they are unknown to us we have one of the greatest treats in store in making their acquaintance, and probably the most convenient form for this purpose is Percy's *Reliques of Ancient English Poetry*, a volume easily obtainable.

As a link with the studies we have to pursue among more modern poets we shall close this present section with a reference to the famous poem of Thomas Gray, written in 1751. It at once obtained popularity, and has not failed to hold the heart of the people since that time. It was the work of a poet who in his other writings scarcely touches the popular mind at all. He was a student and a most fastidious recluse. But one evening in the churchyard of Stokes Poges opened his heart to the meaning of much that is deepest and most universal in human experience, and he was enabled to express it in clear, exquisite and touching language, so that all could feel its power. The lines may be so familiar as to require no quotation, but we may at least enjoy some of them once more together, and remember that the tragedy of much of the democracy of the past it is one of our endeavours to remove, and that if what was true of the middle of the eighteenth century is not so true to-day, the Adult School Movement has played not an inconspicuous part in lifting the veil of ignorance from many minds, and making it possible for them to take more effective part in the life of the community. It may well be that Gray's own verses have had their share in rousing men and women to such service.

> " Some village Hampden, that with dauntless breast
>   The little tyrant of his fields withstood ;
> Some mute inglorious Milton here may rest,
>   Some Cromwell guiltless of his country's blood.
>
> " But knowledge to their eyes her ample page,
>   Rich with the spoils of time, did ne'er unroll ;
> Chill Penury repressed their noble rage,
>   And froze the genial current of the soul."*

* Percy's *Reliques*, or the volumes of ballads in the Canterbury Poets should be consulted. 1s. each.

CHAPTER IV—OLIVER GOLDSMITH AND WILLIAM COWPER.

THERE is no need in the present instance to sketch the lives of the poets with whom we deal, since the facts are either familiar or easily accessible.

The first of the two poets had a very varied experience, and knew at firsthand so many forms of life—in the house of his father—a poor Irish clergyman—a penniless student at the university in Dublin—a strolling musician on the Continent of Europe—an apothecary—a doctor—a school master—a man of letters, reckoning among his friends the greatest writers and artists of the day, that he had ample material on which to draw.

Only two of his poems here concern us—the one a picture of the village in which he was reared, and the other, reflections born of his travels abroad.

In his study of *The Deserted Village* we see how his warm heart pierced the cloaks in which men wrap themselves, and penetrated to the common feelings of humanity which touch alike rich and poor, lettered and unlettered.

He paints for us his father's house as a place of shelter for all sorts and conditions of men—the beggar, the ruined spendthrift, the broken soldier.

> " Pleased with his guests, the good man learned to glow,
>   And quite forgot their vices in their woe ;
>   Careless their merits or their faults to scan
>   His pity gave ere charity began."

The schoolmaster and the innkeeper live again in the tender lines. He pictures all these scenes and then contrasts them with the present ruined condition of the place—a ruin brought about by the thoughtless selfishness of the rich.

> " The rich man's joys increase, the poor's decay,
>   'Tis yours to judge how wide the limits stand
>   Between a splendid and happy land."

He was as conscious of the burdens and bale of unjust land laws as we are to-day, and his lines may yet fire many a speech destined to set free those whom these laws hold in bondage. Enforced emigration has deprived the hamlet of its richest blood, as is so often the case even now. As he thinks of all the misery entailed he calls on the poetic Muse to aid him and to wing his message to many hearts.

> " Teach erring man to spurn the rage of gain,
>   Teach him, that states of native strength possessed,
>   Though very poor, may still be very blessed."

In *The Traveller* we have an attempt to note the various temperaments and gifts of the inhabitants of the countries described, so that again the poem is a timely one, since it teaches us that first lesson of Internationalism, the need of understanding and entering into sympathethic relations with our neighbours. He does not praise with unstinting voice; nay, rather, he views with something akin to prejudice the peoples whose life he paints. Yet are his methods sound, and he has the credit of going beyond the men of his age in the endeavour to lead his countrymen to view men of other nations with new eyes. The poem concludes with a treatment of Freedom in which he sounds the wise note of moderation—if freedom is to be at all it must be the portion of all, and not of one section of the community, who " Call it freedom, when themselves are free." Once more he returns to the theme that had been burned into his heart in rural Ireland, and bewails the desolation where had once been plenty. His last word is as pertinent to-day as when it was written, that true freedom must be sought and found within our souls.

> " Still to ourselves is every place consigned,
> Our own felicity we make or find."

William Cowper stands almost alone in the ranks of our English poets. He owes little to his predecessors, and he is not strong enough to be a pioneer; yet he holds with either hand, one might say, to the more formal teaching spirit of the eighteenth century and to the new attitude towards men and nature found in the great outburst of the poetry of the nineteenth century.

For our present purpose his verse concerns us because of three features rightly noted in it by one of his critics : " a tender and kindly interest in the simple domestic affections ; a sense of the brotherhood of man ; a horror of cruelty or vice." These are feelings which draw him close to the heart of the democracy, and make him one with it.

Cowper has remained a poet widely read by those who care little for other schools of verse, and in many homes of the people otherwise ignorant of the great poets his works are known and loved. There is much quiet humour which endears him to the ordinary reader, for he touches up our common frailties, as in this passage —descriptive of a type of conversation not yet extinct.

> " Some men employ their health—an ugly trick—
> In making known how oft they have been sick,
> And give us in recitals of disease
> A doctor's trouble, but without the fees :
>
> *   *   *   *   *
>
> They thought they must have died, they were so bad ;
> Their peevish hearers almost wish they had."

He was a sincere, but not a blind patriot, and has well put in a couple of lines the attitude that many of us must adopt at the present moment in our country's history. We cannot leave the whole tasks of patriotism to those in high places, for most of us may say, with him, it

> " was never meant my task ;
> But I can feel thy fortunes and partake
> Thy joys and sorrows with as true a heart."

He hates all slavery and prays

> " that where Britain's power
> Is felt, mankind may feel her mercy too."

In such a poem as *Expostulation* he lays bare, with no shrinking hand, the follies and sins of his country, and it is well worth re-reading to-day. He is the servant of truth, and that is no vain boast for any man—so can all be the best helpers of the State.

> " Truth alone—where'er my life be cast :
> In scenes of plenty, or the pining waste—
> Shall be my chosen theme, my glory to the last."

It is not difficult to make sport of much of Cowper's verse, and a good deal of it is intolerably dull, but some of the most healthful influences on our modern life are to be found there, and at least those who find other poetry difficult will find his easy, and a suitable introduction to more varied forms of poetic expression. And to read him will render us a still greater service, for we shall learn from him the true secret of freedom.

As Stopford Brooke has said : " He struck the first note of the revolutionary poetry. He struck it in connection with God, and with us it has never lost that connection." The lines are among his noblest to which reference is here made, and they prove that he had the wider and fuller vision of the brotherhood of nations.

> "He is the freeman who the truth makes free,
> And all are slaves beside.
> He is indeed a freeman.   Free by birth
> Of no mean city,   planned or ere the hills
> Were built, the fountains opened, or the sea
> With all its roaring multitude of waves.
> His freedom is the same in every state."

Macaulay notes a very beautiful feature in his character—namely, the constancy of his friendship. When Warren Hastings was violently abused on all hands—the poet, who had not met him since his schooldays, wrote lines that show he had trust in the underlying goodness of his old playmate, and will not give ear to the universal abuse. " Cowper," says Macaulay, " had preserved in no common measure the innocence of childhood." It is this quality that makes him so fine an interpreter of many aspects of human life, and nowhere is its beauty more evident than in the famous lines on his mother's portrait ; where a pure tender love reminiscent of childhood abides in the man, and sweetens all memories with contentment.

His love of animals is well known from the charming record he has left of his tame hares.   In his poems this trait of noble characters is also found, and thought for the good of animals is one of the great marks of a truly democratic mind. Without this there can be no real brotherhood, for they are included in a true view of nature. So he writes :

> " I would not enter on my list of friends,
>   (Though graced with polished manners and fine sense,
>   Yet wanting sensibility), the man
>   Who needlessly sets foot upon a worm . . .
>   Ye, therefore, who love mercy, teach your sons
>   To love it too."

This leads him on to re-paint the prophet's picture of the world at peace, and all creatures harmless, and then he bursts forth in high hopes of that fulfilment, proving that he recognised the kind of society in which these ideals would be fulfilled.

> " Where violence shall never lift the sword,
>   Nor cunning justify the poor man's wrong,
>   Leaving the poor no remedy but tears.
>   Where he that fills an office, shall esteem
>   Th' occasion it presents of doing good
>   More than the perquisite."

Cowper was not blind to the errors and mistakes of his own day, and has frequent caustic criticisms on the follies and sins of the society in which he lived. He deals with common relationships and common duties, and is always worthy our consideration in what he has to say about the humblest tasks of life, as well as about its highest opportunities. To him religion—as somewhat narrowly interpreted—was the supreme reality, and he preaches doctrines a good deal too much for the good of his poetry or the pleasure of his readers. But through all, from his earliest verse to his latest, his instinct is sound for the noblest ideals, and we may well believe his own boast to be true :

" O liberty ! the pris'ner's pleasing dream,
 The poet's muse, his passion and his theme,
 Genius is thine, and thou art fancy's nurse,
 Lost without thee, th' ennobling pow'rs of verse,
 Heroic song from thy free touch acquires
 Its clearest tone, the rapture it inspires ;
 Place me where winter breathes its keenest air,
 And I will sing if liberty be there ;
 And I will sing at liberty's dear feet,
 In Afric's torrid clime, or India's fiercest heat."*

* Goldsmith and Cowper are both issued in the " Canterbury Poets."
1s. each.

CHAPTER V.—GEORGE CRABBE.

IN the subject of this sketch we have a poet who stands midway between the old movement and the new. To some extent he tried to pour the new wine into the old wineskins, and for that reason has remained in comparative neglect for succeeding generations. His model was Pope and the school of poets that, with less mastery than their leader, used the " heroic couplet." Occasionally, as we shall see, Crabbe broke away from that monotonous rhythm, but, in the main, he clung to it, and it was not a very suitable medium for his new message. During his life-time new forces were at work, and he lived long enough to be contemporary with, though largely untouched by those who were breaking away from the past, and heralding the ideas and forms of the new century. Cowper, Scott, Wordsworth and Coleridge were in the ascendant before his last poems were issued. For many years his muse was silent, but the last period of his poetic activity was in some ways less in touch with the democracy than his earlier efforts.

He went through a hard school in his youth, and his own experiences enabled him to realise in large measure the lot in life of those about whom he sang.

He was born in Aldeborough, Suffolk, in 1754. His father seems to have been a man of curious temper. Given to drink and low company on the one hand, yet, on the other, a lover of poetry, and accustomed to read aloud to his family the verse of Milton and Young. He saw the advantages of education and did his best to give his son George the utmost benefits in that direction that were in his power.

Yet, for his best work, the boy's best school seems to have been the open air—his walks by the sea-shore and on the moor—and his constant association with all sorts and conditions of men on the wharf, and in the little town. He got to know intimately the life of the poor and labouring classes, and even for some time, owing to his father's falling fortunes, had to work as little better than a day labourer among the butter-tubs on the quay. This, in spite of the fact, that he had already gone a certain way in his professional studies as a doctor, and in accordance with the fashion of the time, had begun to practice, for he had served years of apprenticeship under a surgeon at Woodbridge. While here he had already met the lady who was afterwards his wife, and her steady, bright, sympathetic love was a guiding star to him in these dark years. He had already begun his work as a poet, for in 1775 he published a satire called *Inebriety*. This was rather a sorry performance in itself, but showed the direction of his mind towards serious social problems, and the dedication of his gift towards the uplift of man's ideals.

His scientific studies led him to devote much time to botany, and his later verse bears many

traces of his love of wild flowers, even if sometimes the lines are rather suggestive of a florist's
catalogue ! He opened the eyes of men for the
first time to the beauties that were at their feet,
and common to every observer, who cared to study
and love them. In his own gardens, throughout
his life, he planted all common and uncommon
herbs that he found on his walks, in order that
they might be under his observation. The
straightforward simplicity and accuracy of his
description the following lines from the *Village*
prove :

> " There poppies nodding, mock the hope of toil,
>   There the blue bugloss paints the sterile soil,
>   Hardy and high, above the slender sheaf,
>   The shiny mallow waves her silky leaf ;
>   O'er the young shoots the charlock throws a shade,
>   And clasping tares cling round the sickly blade ;
>   With mingled tints the rocky coasts abound,
>   And a sad splendour vainly shines around."

Description of another aspect of nature is
interesting for its own sake, as showing the care
of his observation, but further, because it is his
own account of the next, and most important
step in his history :—

> " As on the neighbouring beach yon swallows stand,
>   And wait for favouring winds to leave the land ;
>   While still for flight the ready wing is spread,
>   So waited I the favouring hour and fled."

The flight was to London in 1870 with three
pounds in his pocket, and a letter of introduction

from his lady-love to a linen-draper's wife in Cornhill.

Then began struggles with poverty in earnest, frequent visits to the pawnbroker, and sometimes only a shilling or two between him and starvation. After trying one and another of the patrons of literature he sent some of his verses to Edmund Burke, and it is said that the lines just quoted were among those that convinced the great statesman he had discovered another poet. Anyone who recognises the true spirit of poetry will understand why the simplicity and genuine first-hand observation that characterises the lines gave the critic his certainty of conviction. From that hour onwards Burke stood his friend, and was the main factor in his progress from unknown poverty to a position of recognition in society and of comfort in his new profession. At first he was private chaplain to the Duke of Rutland— a position that did not well suit his independent temper, though his patron was extremely kind.

Crabbe's marriage to the lady he had so long and faithfully loved took place in 1783, and soon afterwards they moved to Strathern in Leicestershire. Thence he moved to Muston in the same county, where he remained over twenty-five years. His striking poem, *Sir Eustace Grey*, was the next important effort of his muse. It is the picture of a mind deranged—the dreams that come to a man in such a condition—the comforts of religion to his soul and the pathetic lines of farewell to his visitors—lines that were applied by Sir Walter Scott to himself on his departure to Italy, when he was sadly conscious that his own mental powers were failing.

> " Must you, my friends, no longer stay ?
>   Thus quickly all my pleasures end ;
> But I'll remember, when I pray,
>   My kind physician and his friend ;
> And those sad hours you deign to spend
>   Wirh me, I shall requite them all ;
> Sir Eustace for his friends shall send,
>   And thank their love at Greyling Hall."

To old themes he returned in *The Parish Register*, the reminiscences of an old clergyman as he looks over the records of those he has baptised, married, and buried. Nothing could be more simply human, and it takes genius to make poetry of such material. He pictures the village on its bright side with great beauty, and on its dark side with stern realism.

> " Here, in cabal, a disputatious crew
>   Each evening meet : the sot, the cheat, the shrew ;
> Riots are nightly heard."

Dark stories of sorrow alternate with brighter pictures of village virtue—and the life-history of simple heroes and heroines, who let their day's work reveal their worth, like that of the parish clerk.

> " I feel his absence in the hours of prayer,
>   And view his seat, and sigh for Isaac there ;
> I see no more those white locks thinly spread
> Round the bald polish of that honoured head,

*   *   *   *   *

> No more that meek and suppliant look in prayer,
> Nor the pure faith (to give it force) are there,—
> But he is blest, and I lament no more
> A wise, good man, contented to be poor."

He followed this poem with one entitled *The Borough*, intended as a picture, " extended and magnified," as Canon Ainger says, " of the town he knew so well, Aldeburgh." It is a remote and unregarded town—its vicar a votary of things as they are :—

> " Habit with him was all the test of truth ;
> ' It must be right ; I've done it from my youth.'
> Questions he answered in as brief a way ;
> ' It must be wrong—it was of yesterday.' "

The poet's sympathy with the need of better conditions for the people is revealed in these satiric lines :—

> " Here our reformers come not ; none object
> To paths polluted, or upbraid neglect ;
> None care that ashy heaps at doors are cast,
> That coal dust flies along the blinding blast ;
> None heed the stagnant pools on either side,
> Where new launched ships of infant sailors ride ;
> Rodneys in rags here British valour boast,
> And lisping Nelsons fight the Gallic coast."

There are idylls of extreme beauty, tales of exquisite pathos in his pages, and many passages revealing a true apprehension of the beauty of nature, and the gift of interpretation that was new in literature. Evidences cannot be given here, for the best in Crabbe is only found in longer extracts that can find place in these pages. This is not matter for regret if readers will only seek them there for themselves ! Let one short quotation suffice to show the manner of his dealing with the finest traits of character he paints :

> "I know not if they live
> With all the comforts wealth and plenty give,
> But with pure joy to envious souls denied,
> To suppliant meanness and suspicious pride ;
> And village maids of happy couples say,
> ' They lived like Jesse Bourn and Colin Grey."

His pioneer work as a social reformer lay largely in his suggestiveness of the misery of existing conditions, that brought home to many minds the imperative need of alteration. How better could the monotony of the typical Workhouse be shown than thus :

> " What, if no grievous fears their lives annoy,
> Is it not worse no prospects to enjoy ?
> 'Tis cheerless living in such bounded view,
> With nothing dreadful, but with nothing new,
> Nothing to bring them joy, to make them weep,
> The day itself is, like the night, asleep."

One of his best known works is a volume that appeared in 1812, under the simple title, *Tales*. They are almost entirely founded on events personally known to the writer, and thus have a directness and power that otherwise might have been lacking in a poet whose imaginative gift is not very great. The Tales are sometimes tragic, and most have a clearly designed moral lesson, and have consequently appealed to many eager students of ethics like Newman and Bishop

Gore. Sometimes a lighter touch brightens the book, as in the quaint and sly humour of *The Frank Courtship*, the close of which is an admirable example of succinct verse telling adequately its story without a word too much. It is the conversation between father and daughter, after an interview between herself and the lover chosen for her by her parents. In that period the young people had learned to respect one another, but not yet to go much further. The father fears all is lost, and thus chides the maid :

> " ' Then hear me, Sybil; should Josiah leave
> Thy father's house ! ' ' My father's child would grieve.'
> ' That is of grace, and if he come again
> To speak of love ? ' ' I might from grief refrain.'
> ' Then wilt thou, daughter, but design embrace ? '—
> ' Can I resist it if it be of grace ? '
> ' Dear child ! in three plain words thy mind express,
> ' Wilt thou have this good youth ? ' ' Dear father, yes.' "

The Tales of the Hall (1819) was the last work published during his life-time, and contain some of his finest work, though the interest in the simpler aspects of life has somewhat faded, and the democratic tone is somewhat dimmed. " He was a dispeller of many illusions," says one of his biographers, and that we know is a great service, but he was also an awakener of new interests. Nature, the common life of man, the simplicities and realities of life, he saw their beauty and their power, and he led men to make the most of the opportunities afforded them, and to give new values to experience. His pictures, if sometimes too grey, are in the main truthful and touching, and he raises within us admiration for the highest and truest elements in life. To read Crabbe is to become more tolerant towards life's failures, more severe against all falsehood, and more tender in our judgment of others' faults, while more stern with ourselves.*

* Selections from Crabbe are published in the Canterbury Poets 1/-. The Oxford edition is the most convenient and inexpensive (2/-) of the complete poems.

CHAPTER VI.—ROBERT BURNS.

THOUGH Robert Burns was a contemporary of Cowper and Crabbe and a keen and appreciative student of Gray, we enter a quite different atmosphere when we turn from their pages to his poems. In the case of Gray and Cowper they were at best sympathetic outside observers of the life of the classes they describe, but Burns knew in his own person the hard lot of poverty, and the daily struggle with the unfriendly soil from which his bread had to be won. He stands for all time as the interpretation of the Scottish peasant, who reveres his work next almost to the Bible. But it is not the Scottish peasant alone, but the universal heart of humanity that finds its experience echoed in the lines of the Ayrshire ploughman. Not only his fellow men, but the voice of nature he was able to catch and to render clear to other ears, who else had been deaf to its music. This is recognised in Longfellow's fine tribute—a poem far too little known for its exquisite understanding of his brother bard.

> " I see amid the fields of Ayr
> A ploughman, who, in foul and fair,
>   Sings at his task
> So clear, we know not if it is
> The laverock's song we hear, or his,
>   Nor care to ask.
>
> *   *   *   *
>
> But still the music of his song
> Rises o'er all elate and strong;
>   Its master chords

> Are Manhood, Freedom, Brotherhood,
> Its discords but an interlude
> Between the words."

For our present purpose all the other tempting aspects of his poetry must be disregarded, and we must concentrate our attention upon the significance of these " master-chords."

One of the most striking notes in Burns, whether we consider his writings or his personal character, is sincerity. He hides nothing—least of all his faults. It may seem to some that he intrudes the latter and boasts of his sins and frailties. At any rate, he does not cloak them, and nothing raises his wrath so strongly as hypocrisy. His most bitter satire is directed against it—his sympathy with the devil himself seems partly born out of the idea that anyhow there was no hiding *his* evil ! He cries

> " God knows, I'm no the thing I should be,
> Nor am I even the thing I could be,
> But twenty times I rather would be
> An atheist clean
> Than under gospel colours hid be
> Just for a screen."

For him the honour and gifts of all the world are, in themselves, of no account.

> " The rank is but the guinea's stamp
> The man's the gowd for a' that."

" The honest man," " the man o' independent mind," " The pith o' sense an' pride o' worth," it is for these things he supremely cares. Let man stand stripped of all adventitious aids, and Burns will value him for what he is. He was not blind to social and other advantages, but even when he mingled with the worldly great, it was the man himself that attracted them, and to such real men whatever their station the poet was himself drawn. Among his correspondents were many in much higher social position than himself, but he does not cringe before them, he talks to them as to fellow men and women.

Thus from his *Elegy on Captain Matthew Henderson* we may take these lines :

> " Go to your scriptur'd tombs, ye Great,
> In a' the tinsel trash o' state ;
> But by the honest turf I'll wait,
> Thou man of worth !
> And weep the ae best fellow's fate
> E'er lay in earth."

In humorous verse he records his first social meeting with " a lord " in Edinburgh society, and closes with the lines :

> " The fient a pride, nae pride had he,
> Nor sauce, nor state, that I could see
> Mair than an honest ploughman."

No man ever loved the thought of freedom more than he. It rings with a triumphant note through all his song. He loved it because he knew its secret in his own soul. In his fine autobiographical poem he sings :

> " But cheerful still, I am as well as a monarch in a palace, O,
>   Tho' Fortune's frown still hunts me down, with all her wonted
>   malice, O ;
>   I make indeed my daily bread, but ne'er can make it farther, O,
>   But as daily bread is all I need, I do nor much regard her, O."

Here are lines that speak home to our hearts, for they embody the very ideals of education for which we are striving, and inspire in that struggle for real liberty in which it is our highest joy to take our part.

> " Here's freedom to them that wad read,
>   Here's freedom to them that wad write,
>   There's none ever fear'd that the truth should be heard
>   But they whom the truth would indict ! "

His love of liberty made him an ardent supporter of the French Revolution, even when such sympathy caused him to run considerable risks that he could ill afford. His stirring verses on *The Tree of Liberty* are too long to quote, but should be known to us all, and they are a very appropriate message at the present hour, when we find ourselves the allies of that nation, who more than a hundred years ago planted it in the soil of France.

> " This fruit is worth a' Afric's wealth ;
>   To comfort us 'twas sent, man,
>   To gie the sweetest blush o' health
>   And mak' us a' content, man."

Better known, though not more significant is his great song, " *Scots, wha hae wi' Wallace bled*," William Wallace was throughout life his great

hero, and he tells how as a lad, worn with his
week's work at the plough, he used willingly to
devote the hours of his only day of rest to long
pilgrimages on foot to the scenes of his hero's
career.

But there were other battles of freedom that
Burns fought, and into the heritage so won we
also have entered. He was one of the great
factors in the broadening of theological and
religious thought. He helped his countrymen,
and through them the world, to realise the
impossible views of God and His dealings with
men harboured in much of their current
theories. More than many learned treatises
did Burns' picture in Satan's den in *Tam o'
Shanter* of

> " Twa span long wee, unchristened bairns "

cause men to revolt against the hideous super-
stition that the Father in Heaven could doom the
innocent to perdition ; it helped to bring them
back to the interpretation of the will of God in
Christ. There can be no divorce between ethics
and religion, that he felt to be a sheet anchor of
man's faith—

> " The fear o' hell's a hangman's whip
> To haud the wretch in order ;
> But where ye feel your honour grip,
> Let that aye be your border ; "

and nowhere more finely is the kernel of this
faith expressed than in the lines :

> " Then at the balance let's be mute,
>   We never can adjust it ;
> What's done we partly may compute,
>   But know not what's resisted."

Into the hands of such a God he was not afraid
to yield even his sin-stained soul.

> " Where with intention I have erred,
>   No other plea I have,
> But, Thou art good, and Goodness still
>   Delighteth to forgive."

It was, as Stopford Brooke remarks, the awful
condemnation of the Christianity around him that
" the Christian ministers of Ayrshire had blotted
out Christ for Burns, and threw him back
unhelped upon himself."

It was natural that such a man should be a
prophet of Brotherhood. He was a strong
Nationalist. No one had sung the praise of
Scotland with such power, or bred such a race of
patriots. Is there any other poet whose name-
day evokes annual speeches and convivial gatherings in his honour, as Burns' day brings Scotsmen
together all over the world ? The love of his
land and of his people breathes through every
page, and he has nothing to say of Internationalism. Yet has he the only sane soil in which
that plant of later development may grow.
Nations must understand their own call and
realise their own opportunity before they learn to
work for others. And Burns oversteps nation-
ality in his great love for man as man. He has

given at least two great songs to universal brotherhood, that many nations have adopted as their
own,

> " For a' that, an' a' that,
>   It's coming yet for a' that,
> That man to man the world o'er
>   Shall brithers be for a' that."

and *Auld Lang Syne*.

This sketch, so short and so imperfect, must
conclude with reference to another great service
rendered by Burns to the democracy of the
world, and with the proof of how its origin was
also democratic—I mean his work as a song-
writer.

It would not be too much to claim that no
song-writer is more famous or has reaped such
reward from his labours as he. Yet recent
research has proved that Burns received the
suggestion for many of his most famous songs in
the verses that were the heritage of his people.
Sometimes it was but the hint of a poem—" the
right lyrical idea," as Henley calls it—sometimes
it was a whole song, which he re-wrote, and in
re-writing transformed. " It is fair to say that
what is best in them is sublimated and glorified
by him, it is also fair to say that but for them
he could never have approved himself the most
exquisite artist in folk-song the world has seen."
Only those who know the sources from which
he drew can understand the enormous service
which he rendered by giving us the songs we all can

sing in pure pleasure and joy. Can the democracy have a greater gift ? No poet, certainly, can give it more, and thus Burns demands our study and our love, even if, at times, his language be difficult to master, and at others we find on him " such stains,"

> " as when a Grace
> Sprinkles another's laughing face
> With nectar, and runs on."

---

* The best poems of Burns appear in two volumes of the Canterbury Poets. 1s. each.

WILLIAM WORDSWORTH.

CHAPTER VII.
WILLIAM WORDSWORTH.

WHEN we come to deal with Wordsworth we are considering a name without which the England of our generation would not be what it is. He has been one of the greatest factors in moulding the present-day outlook upon nature and our fellow men. There are poets who speak only to the students of literature, or whose work concerns only the lovers of their art, but who do not touch the great stream of the world's life, but Wordsworth is not one of these. He has even introduced a word into the language, as did Plato, Socrates, Shakespeare, and other great masters, and to term one a "Wordsworthian," is to express certain clearly understood characteristics about his attitude to life. He has expressed this feeling a thousand times but never better than in his lines on *Yarrow Revisited :*

> " Eternal blessings on the Muse,
>   And her divine employment !
> The blameless Muse, who trains her sons
>   For hope and calm enjoyment ;
> Albeit sickness, hungering yet,
>   Has o'er their pillow brooded ;
> And care waylays their steps—a sprite
>   Not easily eluded."

Much more familiar are the lines that reveal the Wordsworthian's spirit in perfection—that spirit which traces in every sight of Nature a revelation of the Mind that lies behind Nature, and renders it an expression of Divine realities.

" My heart leaps up when I behold
    A rainbow in the sky ;
So was it when my life began,
So is it now I am a man ;
So be it when I shall grow old,
    Or let me die !
The child is father of the man,
I could wish my days to be
Bound each to each by natural piety."

These lines bring before us another great feature of his poetry, namely, the simplicity of his language. There is not a word in them that is not familiar. His democratic tendency is nowhere more visible than in his theory of true poetic diction. He revolted against much of the artificial and involved expression of his predecessors. His aim was to take the language of the common people and make it the vehicle of poetry, and he succeeded. Of him it has been truly said, " His poetry is sincere, we can trust it ; it is lucid, we can understand it ; it is original, there is nothing elsewhere like it in the world." He sought to reproduce that language that flows from men's lips, as the sincere utterance of their hearts, but in its highest and best moments. It was when purged by sorrow, cleansed by repentance, fired by love, chastened by sympathy, heightened by visions of the unseen, that he caught it, and transfused it into undying verse. As Pater truly says in his wonderful *Appreciation*, " He chooses to depict people from humble life, because, being nearer to nature than others, they are on the whole more impassioned, certainly more direct in their expression of passion, that he values their humble words. It was not for their tameness but for this passionate sincerity, that he chose incidents and situations from common life, ' related in a selection of language really used by men.' He constantly endeavours to bring his language near to the real language of men ; to the real language of men, not on the dead level of their ordinary intercourse, but in select moments of vivid sensation, when the language is winnowed and ennobled by excitement." In proof of this, let us read such poems as *We are Seven, Alice Fell, The Pet Lamb, Michael,* and any narrative in *The Excursion,* and we shall find how true it is.

Wordsworth became the revealer of his own dalesmen, because his heart was with them, and he understood their inward life. As he writes himself, at the close of *The Two Thieves,* revealing this secret,

> " Old man ! whom so oft I with pity have eyed,
> I love thee, and love the sweet Boy at thy side ;
> Long yet mayst thou live ! for a teacher we see
> That lifts up the veil of our nature in thee."

And thus it comes to pass that his religion has the true democratic ring about it also. He loved to worship in the church at Grasmere, among his own country-folk, but religion was not for him bounded by walls or creeds. His *Labourer's Noonday Hymn* utters his most inmost convictions.

> " Each field is then a hallowed spot,
> An altar is in each man's cot,
> A church in every grove that spreads
> Its living roof above our heads."

Wordsworth's youth was one with the new-found power of the democracy in Europe, and the thrill of it drew from him those oft-quoted and unforgettable lines :

> " Bliss was it in that dawn to be alive,
> But to be young was very heaven."

On French soil the song of liberty seemed universal. Not only did the lips of her sons and daughters sing it, and the clarion tones of her trumpets proclaim it, but :

> " Methought from every cot the watchful bird
> Burned with ear-piercing power till then unheard ;
> Each clashing mill, that broke the murmuring streams
> Rocked the charmed thought in their delightful dreams ;
> The measured echo of the distant flail
> Wound in more welcome cadence down the vale ;
> With more majestic course the water rolled,
> And ripening foliage shone with richer gold."

The pages of that wonderful, though somewhat difficult autobiographical poem, *The Prelude*, are full of the same ideals (see especially Books 9 to 11). He was full of the dream of the day when he

> " as sum and crown of all
> Should see the people have a strong hand
> In framing their own laws ;   whence better days
> To all mankind."

And even when these fair hopes were for the time being wrecked, Wordsworth did not lose his faith in these high and noble ideals, but continued to cherish his heart upon them, and to bid his own country look to Freedom, Justice, Love and Pity as her greatest possessions. There is no reading more stimulating, heartening and uplifting in these days in which we live than are his great sonnets and other poems dedicated to *National Independence and Liberty*, and to *Liberty and Order*. Let us remind ourselves of some of the great lines, and noble messages they contain :

> " Wisdom doth live with children round her knees ;
> Books, leisure, perfect freedom, and the talk
> Man holds with week-day man in the hourly walk
> Of the mind's business ; these are the degrees
> By which true sway doth mount."

> " Thou hast great allies ;
> Thy friends are exultations, agonies,
> And love, and man's unconquerable mind."

> " We must be free or die ; who speak the tongue
> That Shakespeare spake ; the faith and morals hold
> Which Milton held."

> " We are selfish men
> Oh raise us up, return to us again
> And give us manners, virtue, freedom, power,"

> " The prophecy—like that of this wild blast,
> Which, while it makes the heart with sadness shrink
> Tells also of bright colours that shall succeed."

> ' Say, what is Honour ? 'Tis the finest sense
> Of justice which the human mind can frame."

> " Have we not conquered ? by the vengeful sword ?
> Ah, no, by dint of magnanimity."

> " Is not conscience ours,
> And truth, whose eye guilt only can make dim,
> And will, whose office, by divine command,
> Is to control and check disordered powers ! "

These must suffice to show us how much there is to be found in Wordsworth's poems of this order to guide us to the highest and noblest ideals of democracy. Nor have I quoted such better known poems as *The Ode to Duty* or *The Happy Warrior*.

In other ways, scarcely less striking, did he show his real sympathy with the democracy, notably in his splendid plea for education, to be found in the ninth book of *The Excursion*. His basis for it is not only truly democratic, but truly religious.

> " The primal duties shine aloft—like stars ;
> The charities that soothe, and heal, and bless,
> Are scattered at the feet of man—like flowers,
> The generous inclination, the just rule,
> Kind wishes, and good actions, and pure thoughts.
> No mystery is here."

Then follows the great apostrophe—too long to quote, but which should be carefully studied by every reader—beginning :

> " Oh for the coming of that glorious time,
> When, prizing knowledge as her noblest wealth
> And best protection"

England may see to it that all her people share in its privileges. Not yet have we risen to that ideal, but Wordsworth has himself been the inspirer of many who have worked hard within

the limits of existing movements, and may yet
inspire many more among us, if we will but drink
at his springs.

There is a deeper direction still in which
Wordsworth is democratic, and that has been
again splendidly indicated by Walter Pater. It
is by showing us " the supreme importance of
contemplation   in   the   conduct   of   life."
" Wordsworth, and other poets who have been like
him in ancient and modern times, are the masters,
the experts, in this art of impassioned contemplation. Their work is to withdraw the
thoughts for a little from the mere machinery of
life, to fix them, with appropriate emotions, on the
spectacle of those great facts in man's existence
which no machinery affects, ' of the great and
universal passions of men,' the most general and
interesting of their occupations, and the entire
world of nature—on the operations of the
elements, and the appearances of the visible
universe, in storm and sunshine, on the revo-
lutions of the seasons, in cold and heat, in loss of
friends and kindred, or injuries and resentments,
on gratitude and hope, on fear and sorrow."
This is what Wordsworth designed, and what in
large measure he accomplished.   He accomplished
it because he possessed, as few have done

> " that inward eye
> Which is the bliss of solitude."

But tuition under his guidance and patient
observance of his methods will improve the

powers of our inward vision, and enable us to find
in Nature and in man in contact with Nature,
something of the strength, the help, the uplift
he found.   Time we must have for the nurture of
our highest nature, and the more we can learn
of the lesson of contemplation the more perfectly
will we gain possession of our souls.   If we
company awhile with his men and women we may
learn, as he did, our greatest lessons from the
humblest.   In taking leave of his leech-gatherer
he cried :

> " I could have laughed myself to scorn to find
>   In that decrepit man so firm a mind,
>   ' God,' said I, ' be my help and stay secure ;
>   I'll think of the Leech-gatherer on the lonely moor ! ' "

So may we.   And further, Wordsworth will be
one of our best teachers in unlocking the hearts
of others that we may become sharers in their
secret, and so heighten the level of their common
life, and bring it nearer to God's purpose for the
world.   His is a poetry, which, as Professor
Dixon has said, " is able to look facts in the face,
and at the same time persuade us that our true
life is greater than we know, and can open for us
sudden and strange vistas until through a gather-
ing sense of awe and majesty we think we know

> " ' The hills where our life rose,
>   And the sea where it goes.' "

There is also a volume of Wordsworth (well selected) in the Canterbury
Poets.

CHAPTER VIII.
THE CORN-LAW RHYMERS.

THE acute consciousness of vivid contrasts is a frequent source of powerful poetry. We have only to think of the Book of Job in order to prove our point. The greatest tragedies of Greek literature sprang from a similar origin—the baffling problems of the world's contradictions. There is a famous passage in one of the mightiest of Latin poets that has put the feeling of this contrast in a marvellous picture.

> " 'Tis sweet when tempests roar upon the sea,
>   To watch from land another's deep distress
> Amongst the waves—his toil and misery ;
>   Not that his sorrow makes our happiness,
> But that some sweetness there must ever be
>   Watching what sorrows we do not possess :
> So, too, 'tis sweet to safely view from far
> Gleam o'er the plains the savage ways of war."

But Lucretius is here on the selfish side of such contrasts—the truest poetry has sprung from the hearts of those on whom the contrasts have pressed heavily, and who have to find some way out of the bitter riddle of life's inequalities.

The England of the early part of the nineteenth century was such a time, and among those on whom these problems pressed most heavily were our people who were the toilers in the land, and who received no adequate reward for their toil. There was added the additional burden of taxed bread, and the effort to remove this injustice was the great motive force of the men whose work we have here to consider.

It was a popular movement into which they threw themselves, and the consciousness that they were attacking only one aspect of a widely present menace gave new power to their plea, and new pathos to their song. We do not claim for them rank as poets alongside those we have hitherto considered, or intend later to discuss, but they have a very important place in carrying on the democratic tradition, and their lines— too readily forgotten—touch many chords in our hearts that may be irresponsive to finely-tuned lyres. As Carlyle writes of one of them, "The works of this Corn Law Rhymer we might liken rather to some little fraction of a rainbow; hues of joy and harmony painted out of troublous tears. No round full bow, indeed, gloriously spanning the heavens, shone on by the full sun ; and with seven-striped gold crimson border(as in some sort the office of poetry) dividing Black from Brilliant : not such, alas, still far from it ! Yet, in very truth, a little prismatic blush growing genuine among the wet clouds ; which proceeds, from a sun-cloud hidden, yet indicates that a sun does shine, and above these vapours, a whole azure vault and celestial firmament stretch serene." He to whom Carlyle thus refers was Ebenezer Elliott, the Sheffield poet, born in 1781, and living till 1849. He had a hard and difficult childhood—not only overshadowed by poverty, but by the hard ultra-Calvinism of his parents' religious ideas. Not till he was twenty-three years of age did he earn any money for himself, as for seven years he gave all his work to his father without a wage. In the midst of all the gloom one star guided him—his love of nature, which, as he tells us, wooed him alike " from ale-house and chapel." Knowing the type of the latter that appealed to his father, we need neither wonder nor regret the alienation.

By the time he was a man of forty brighter days came and the latter part of his life was spent in comparative comfort. His one great purpose was to have the Corn Laws reformed, and he lived to see the desire of his soul. The injustice burned deeply into his inward spirit. " Our labour, our skill, our profits, our hopes, our lives, our children's souls are bread-taxed," he cries, and the consciousness of what it all meant made him a good hater. Like other great souls— Dante, as a conspicuous instance—he would have sung with Newman :

> " And wouldst thou reach, rash scholar mine,
>   Love's high unruffled state ?
> Awake ! thy easy dreams resign,
>   First learn thee how to hate."

Indeed, his own terrible words prove that this was really his experience :

> " They love not God who do not hate man's foes
>   With hatred—not like mine—
> But deep as Hell and blacker. To loathe those
> Who blast the hope of freedom as it blows
>   Is love divine."

We quote the words, and emphasise the experience because in our own day there is a very real danger of many not passing outside the zone of this monstrous shadow, and mistaking it for the light itself.   Hatred can never accomplish divine work, and it is false to suppose it to be the true basis upon which something nobler and better can be builded.   And Elliott himself passed beyond it, as these lines of his prove :

> " Then, Father, will the nations all
>   As with the sound of seas,
> In universal festival
>   . Sing words of joy, like these :
> Let each love all, and all be free,
>   Receiving as they give :
> Lord ! Jesus died for love and Thee,
>   So let Thy children live."

His love of freedom did not cease with his desire to see the liberty of his own countrymen, but many verses breathe the longing for the liberation of oppressed Poland, and these read with added force now, when our people are once more engaged in a struggle that involves the highest hopes of that distressed nation.   His sympathies are also with the first faint stirrings of the woman's movements, and he has visions of a great future for his sisters :

> " And in her garden of the sun
>   Heaven's brightest rose shall bloom,
> For woman's best is unbegun,
>   Her advent yet to come."

In the cruel workshops of that day he hears them singing at their toil :

> " How wildly sweet,
> Like flute-notes in a storm, the psalm ascends,
> From yonder pile, in traffic's dirtiest street."

And like an arrow in his heart rankles the suffering of the children. These were the days when their liberators were only arising, and one of his most poignant, haunting poems takes rank with Mrs. Browning's *Cry of the Children :*

> " Child, is thy father dead ?
>   Father is gone !
> Why did they tax his bread ?
>   God's will be done !
> Mother has sold her bed :
> Better to die than wed !
> Where shall she lay her head ?
>   Home we have none !
>
> " Doctor said air was best,
>   Food we had none :
> Father, with panting breast,
>   Groan'd to be gone :
> Now he is with the blest,
> Mother says death is best !
> We have no place of rest—
>   Yes, we have one !

One of his longest poems, *The Village Patriarch*, shows strong traces of the influence of Crabbe, and its hero, Enoch Wray, is a touching figure. In it, and frequently throughout his work, we trace that love of nature that deepened in expression and joy as life went on. He often rises to the level of the finest interpreters of nature when he touches her least discerned beauties.

> " Blue Eyebright ! loveliest flower of all that grow
> In flower-loved England ! Flower whose hedge-side gaze
> Is like an infant's. What heart doth not know
> Thee, clustered smiles of the bank !

Or again,

> " The lark was in the cloud : the woodbine hung
>   More sweetly o'er the chaffinch while he sung :
> And the wild rose, from every dripping bush,
>   Beheld in silvery sheaf the mirrored blush."

But nothing delights him so much as to think of the toilers sharing all this beauty as their own possession.

> " Sun-waked forest !
>   Bird that soarest
> O'er the mute, empurpled moor !
> Throstle's song, that stream-like flowest,
> Wind, that over dew-drop goest,
> Welcome now the way-worn poor ! "

Turned from the churches of the rich by the haughty pride of the worshippers :

> " Therefore we seek the daisied plain,
>   Or climb the hills, to touch Thy feet,
> Here, far from splendour's city fane,
>   My weary sons and daughters meet. "

And when asked what religion men will there practise, he has a memorable reply :

> " What is Religion ?   Speak the truth in love,
> Reject no good.   Mend, if thou canst, thy lot,
> Doubting, enquire—nor dictate till thou prove,
> Enjoy thy own—exceed not, trespass not,
> Pity the scorners of life's meanest throng,
> If wrong'd, forgive—that Hate may lose its sting,
> Think, speak, work, get—bestow or wisely keep
> So live, that thou mayst smile, and no one weep,
> Be blessed—like birds that sing because they love."

When we next sing his wonderful People's Anthem :

> " When wilt Thou save the people ? "

shall we remember from what a heart it sprang, and put a deeper meaning than before into the prayer, because we know something of the poet ?

An even better known member of the Chartist band was Thomas Cooper. In his home in Gainsborough he drank in the first deep lessons of history and love of freedom in the tomes he found in the forgotten library, of which he tells us with such unfeigned joy in his autobiography. In the Adult School in that town he learned to express himself, and to feel the breath of the new wind that was blowing over England. In the school he opened later at Leicester he and his friends Bramwich and Jones made songs for the people— not very poetic songs, probably, but they were the forerunners of the finer ones we now enjoy in more modern collections. Cooper's longest poem was written in prison, and is a curious work. It is entitled *The Purgatory of Suicides*, but deals with the great question, " Is life worth living ? " and is a strong indictment of all oppressive forces. As Carlyle divined—it possesses " indisputable traces of genius—a dark Titanic energy." It does not lend itself well to quotation, and makes from its length and monotony somewhat dreary reading—yet there are in it touches of beauty, and throughout we can trace the fire of the reformer's zeal. To the Leceister hymn-book Cooper contributed only one hymn, and that not of special excellence, and this he himself quite frankly confesses. Its general idea is somewhat akin to Elliott's much finer production. Its opening lines are these :

> " God of the earth, and sea, and sky,
> To Thee Thy mournful children cry ;
> Didst Thou the blue that bends o'er all
> Spread for a general funeral pall ? "

Throughout the whole movement in which these men were interested there throbbed not only an intense love of Freedom, but a fervent desire for general world-wide Peace, and this is expressed in some stirring lines of Cooper's, which must close this article. They move us more than they ordinarily would in these days in which we are living, when we have seen our own dreams so rudely shattered ; but the prophecy they utter is one that will not fail on our lips, for we too believe that only that Prince of Peace can be the world's final conqueror, and to His cause we dedicate our lives.

> " Truth is growing—hearts are glowing
> With the flame of liberty !
> Light is breaking, thrones are quaking,
> Hark the trumpet of the Free !
> Long, in lowly whispers breathing,
> Freedom wandered drearily,
> Still in faith her laurel wreathing
> For the day when there should be
> Freemen shouting " Victory ! "
>
> *   *   *   *
>
> " Gentle Peace her balm of healing
> On the bleeding world shall pour,
> Brethren love for brethren feeling
> Shall proclaim from shore to shore
> Shout—the sword shall slay no more ! "*

---

* See *Songs of Freedom* in Canterbury Poets 1/-

WALT WHITMAN.

CHAPTER IX—WALT WHITMAN, "THE GOOD GREY POET."

FOR the first time in these studies we treat a poet who was not only a son of the democracy, but for whom the word "democracy" and all it involves was the very burden of his song. He loved to chant "the average man"—or the "divine average" as he sometimes termed him. In a sense in which no one has ever used it more profoundly he might have taken as his motto the line of the Latin poet, "I am a man, and nothing human is reckoned strange to me." Experiences of life about which most men keep the strictest silence were made the subjects of his poems at times, for he could count nothing in life common or unclean that bore upon it the mark of the Divine will for man and woman.

The present writer can never forget the experience, in his university undergraduate days, when Walt Whitman's poetry was first made known to him by a fellow student, and ever since the little volume of selections in the Canterbury Poets has been a cherished companion. The full edition of "Leaves of Grass" is much more easily accessible now than then, and should be in the hands of all who really care to make the full acquaintance of the poet. It will doubtless be a wonderful revelation to those who read its pages for the first time.

On a visit to the United States in 1899, a place of pious pilgrimage was the unlovely and dreary

suburb of Philadelphia, called Camden, where the
poet lived, but he was then too feeble in health
for his admirers to venture on disturbing him
by a visit—an act of self-denial which has been
often seriously regretted since Whitman's death
three years later! His earliest working experience was gained in a printing office, but for many
years his main task was " to loaf and invite his
soul." He lived in intimate communion with
nature, but even more with his fellow men. All
sorts of people interested him, and his greatest
joys were to ride on the top of an omnibus with
the multitudinous life of New York at his feet,
or spend hours on the ferry boats with the crowds
that passed ceaselessly between Brooklyn and
the city.

> " Flow on, river! flow with the flood-tide, and ebb with the ebb-tide !
>   Frolic on, crested and scallop-edg'd waves !
>   Gorgeous clouds of the sunset ! drench with your splendour me, or the
>   men and women generations after me !
>   Cross from shore to shore, countless crowds of passengers !
>   Stand up, tall masts of Mannahatta ! stand up, beautiful hills of
>   Brooklyn !
>   Throb, baffl'd and curious brain ! throw out questions and answers !
>   Suspend here and everywhere, eternal float of solution !
>
>   *   *   *   *   *
>
>   We fathom you not—we love you—there is perfection in you also,
>   You furnish your parts towards eternity,
>   Great or small, you furnish your parts towards the soul."

In these lines we are made familiar with the
strange form Whitman struck out for his new
message. The lines quiver and throb with the
power of old Hebrew poetry. They are not
formless, but obey a law of their own subtle

music. They have not the sound or appearance with which we are accustomed to associate poetry, but, as Mr. Addington Symonds wrote, " Is there no poetry outside the region of rhyme and verse ? Was Sir Philip Sidney so far wrong in his contention that ' apparelled verse is but an ornament and no cause to poetry ; since there have been many most excellent poets that have never versified, and now swarm many versifiers who need never answer to the name of poets ? ' Are we all wrong in thinking that when we read Job, the Psalms, the Prophets, the Song of Solomon, in our English version, we are reading the sublimest, the sweetest, the strongest, the most sensuous poetry that was ever written ? "

Yet he could write the most haunting melody of the more familiar sort, as witness his *O Captain, my Captain*—the wonderful elegy on Abraham Lincoln, which, familiar as it is, must be quoted again, lest any of my readers should not know it

> " O Captain ! my Captain ! our fearful trip is done,
>   The ship has weather'd every rack, the prize we sought is won,
>   The port is near, the bells I hear, the people all exulting,
>   While follow eyes the steady keel, the vessel grim and daring ;
>   But O heart ! heart ! heart !
>   O the bleeding drops of red,
>   Where on the deck my Captain lies,
>   Fallen cold and dead."

Two further verses follow, and the heartbreak of the mourning disciple has never been more poignantly uttered than in this short poem. Again in *The Singer in the Prison* we have an example of the same gift. But by far the mass of his work is written in the unrhymed metre he created, and a little practice will teach us to catch its melody, and to respond to its power, until such poems as *The Mystic Trumpeter*, *When Lilacs last in the Dooryard Bloom'd*, *Pioneers*, *O Pioneers!* and the *Prayer of Columbus* will rank with the most musical of all human songs. As a test of the different methods in which two contemporary poets deal with similar themes let us compare two short poems of Tennyson with two by Whitman. We are all acquainted with the lines

> " Flower in the crannied wall."

Hear what Whitman says :

> " A child said, What is the grass ? fetching it to me with full hands.
> How could I answer the child ? I do not know what it is any more than he.
> I guess it is the handkerchief of the Lord,
> A scented gift and remembrance designedly dropt,
> Bearing the owner's name someway in the corners, that we may see and remark, and say *Whose ?* "

Once more we have his version of the exquisite *Crossing the Bar* :

> " Sail forth, steer for the deep waters only,
> Reckless, O soul, exploring, I with thee, and thou with me,
> For we are bound where mariner has not yet dared to go,
> And we will risk the ship, ourselves and all.
> O my brave soul,
> O farther, farther sail !
> O daring joy, but safe ! are they not all the seas of God.
> O farther, farther, farther sail ! "

In the Civil War Whitman had a great experience as a nurse of wounded and stricken

soldiers, and these days in which we live make the
messages that then welled forth from his heart
all the more poignant. In prose he gave us the
story of that awful war in *Specimen Days in
America* ; in verse the pictures that are etched
in clear and strong lines in the poems called
Drum Taps. These lines live with the lurid light
of reality as we read and re-read them now, and
as we seem to see as he did, in the face of the dead
youth, sacrificing himself for his country

> " I think this face is the face of the Christ Himself,
> Dead and divine and brother of all, and here again He lies."

They have great messages these poems, for
us to-day, for the man that wrote them had
suffered in the agony, and he carried the marks of
his suffering to his grave, but with all their
sadness they throb with hope, and he sees the end
of the fight, and bids his listeners

> " Turn your undying face,
> To where the future, greater than all the past,
> Is swiftly, surely preparing for you."

They are poems of comradeship, and this is
another of his distinctive notes. Democracy
for him is comradeship. The land is to be made
indissoluble

> " With the love of comrades,
> With the life-long love of comrades."

The " city invincible " of which he dreamed,
was to be " the new city of friends."

The word *en-masse* was for him the magic word.
He will not have for himself any gift of which

" all cannot have their counterpart on the same terms." As in the Gospels, so in this man's poems, the master-word is " whoever." Over every head—not of the elect alone—gleams the gold-coloured light of the divine halo. In his prose work *Democratic Vistas*, he has told us what he means. " Did you, too, O friend, suppose Democracy was only for electors, for politics, or for a party name ? I say Democracy is only of use there that it may pass on and come to its flower and fruit in manners, in the highest forms of interaction between men and their beliefs—in Religion, Literature, Colleges, and Schools— Democracy in all public and private life, in the Army and Navy. . . . I submit that the fruition of Democracy on aught like a grand scale, resides altogether in the future." And so he is always summoning us to more heroic effort. This man knew no faintheartedness, nor has he any fear for himself or others, so long as he and they hold their courage aloft with both hands.

He knows just what is needed to make his ideals effective, and he bids us grasp the truth.

> " My comrade !
> For you to share with me two greatnesses—a third one, rising inclusive and more resplendent
> The greatness of love and Democracy—and the greatness of Religion."

He was a man of great faith—faith in his fellows, and in the future of the world, because his faith was so strong in God and in immortality. Not Tennyson preached that Gospel more

earnestly than this man that had lived two years
face to face with death in its most horrible forms.
Few things in literature are more tender and
exquisite, and yet more stimulating, than the
poems contained in the section *Whispers of
Heavenly Death*. He has no doubt—Death
brings life's best answer—it is the harvest of life.

> " Let me glide noiselessly forth :
>   With the key of softness unlock the locks—with a whisper,
>   Set ope the doors, O soul."

And like Tennyson, he was sure also of his Pilot,
though he calls Him by a more tender name
that is characteristic of all his thought—

> " My rendezvous is appointed, it is certain,
>   The Lord will be there, and wait till I come on perfect terms.
>   The great Comrade, the lover true for whom I pine will be there.

Nature to him was no less an expression of
God and so he felt that every man held in his
hands proof that could not be gainsaid of the
spiritual signification of the universe. Visions
of the greatest realities, evidences of the most
profound truths were not withheld from any
son or daughter of men. His democracy was
far-reaching, and the true secret of all life was
at one with and not in contradiction to that
creed.

> " I believe a leaf of grass is no less than the journey work of the stars,
>   And the running blackberry would adorn the parlours of heaven.
>   And a mouse is miracle enough to stagger sextillions of infidels."

There are many aspects of the man and his
message on which one would like to enlarge, but

after all, as Symonds said, the greatest thing is to induce people to study him for themselves. This is the object in all these papers, but in Whitman's case it is more easy than in some, for the great poems are easily accessible—the language is in the main what we can all understand—and he wrote his messages full of love for us—his brothers and sisters of the common life. None of our sins, sorrows, shames, losses, shut us off from that great loving heart. He seeks to share every thought with us, and thus our burden is lifted, and we, too, may become inspired with his optimism, his enthusiasm for humanity, his passion for loving service, and his heroic and triumphant faith.

" Give me, O God, to sing that thought,
    Give me, give him or her I love this quenchless faith,
    In Thy ensemble, whatever else withheld, withhold not from us,
    Belief in plan of Thee enclosed in time and space,
    Health, peace, salvation universal,
    Is it a dream ?

    Nay, but the lack of it the dream,
    And failing it life's lore and wealth a dream,
    And all the world a dream."*

---

* Selections from Whitman in " Canterbury Poets." 1s.

JAMES RUSSELL LOWELL.

CHAPTER X—J. RUSSELL LOWELL.

ONE of the pleasantest memories of student life at the University of Edinburgh in the eighties is that of the week in which took place the Tercentenary Festival. Among the historic celebrations that marked those days none stand out more clearly than the reception given by the students to the famous guests, and of the speeches there delivered not any surpassed in interest that from the lips of Lowell, then Ambassador of the United States at the Court of St. James. His noble, manly bearing, his kind, wonderfully tender eyes and winning words drew all men to him. It is said that once he visited a home, and the maid reported to her mistress, " He didn't leave no card, ma'am, but he had the coaxingest eyes ever you see," and the girl was right and had picked out the unforgettable feature of that face. He spoke to us of the great torchlight procession which he had witnessed a few nights before, and how it suggested to him two ideas—one pathetic the other hopeful. The first was of the endless procession of youth— like that of the bird flying through the lighted hall in the Anglo-Saxon story ; the other that of the ancient torch-race, which suggested to the Latin poet his figure of the lamps of life that pass from hand to hand, and of how the teacher is sometimes permitted to kindle one of these torches. And then his penetrating mind prophesied what we have all found to be true, that the memory of that day would prove a tradition we should all fondly cherish throughout our whole life.

These words were characterisric of the man, of his love for youth, and of his unfailing passion for the living movements around him.

Of the two American poets we have selected to include in this series it would be difficult to find men whose outward lot in life varied more than Lowell's and Whitman's. The one struggling hard with poverty, the other brought up amid every surrounding of comfort—studying at the noblest of his country's universities, and spending part of his life at the courts of kings. Yet both at heart were democrats, and the democratic interest of Lowell's poetry is a permanent element in his message.

Two causes evoked it most clearly—the unjust Mexican campaign of 1846, and the Civil War in which he espoused so warmly the cause of the North, and of the oppressed slaves. Nor is it only that he championed the right on both occasions, but that he saw beneath the surface of current politics and passing quarrels to the eternal principle that all war is an outrage on humanity, and contrary to the law of Christ. Thus it is that the " Biglow Papers " make such excellent reading in the present crisis. Their shrewd humour and caustic sarcasm are undying in their appeal. In the language he chose to be the vehicle of his message we have another testimony to his democratic sympathies. It is the dialect of the common people. To quote his own words, " Thinking the Mexican War, as I think it still, a national crime committed in behoof of slavery, and wishing to put the feeling of those who thought as I did in a way that would tell, I imagined to myself such an up-country man as I had often seen at anti-slavery gatherings, capable of district school English, but always instinctively falling back into the natural stronghold of his homely dialect when heated to the point of self-forgetfulness." This language he has used with inimitable skill, and produced a classic that is loved as much on this side of the Atlantic as on that on which the poems were originally written. Among such riches it is not easy to know where to choose, but we must select a few of the telling passages in order to whet our readers' appetites for more.

> " Ez fer war, I call it murder,—
>> There you hev it plain an' flat ;
> I don't want to go no furder
>> Than my Testyment fer that :
> God hez said so plump an' fairly,
>> It's ez long ez it is broad,
> An' you've got to get up airly
>> Ef you want to take in God.
>
> 'Taint your eppyletts an' feathers
>> Make the thing a grain more right ;
> 'Taint afollerin your bell-wethers
>> Will excuse ye in His sight :
> Ef you take a sword an' dror it,
>> An' go stick a feller thru,
> Guv'ment aint to answer for it,
>> God'll send the bill to you.

> Wot's the use of meetin'-goin' ' !
>   Every Sabbath, wet or dry,
> Ef it's right to go amowin'
>   Feller-men like oats an' rye ?
> I dunno but wut it's pooty
>   Trainin' round in bobtail coats,
> But it's curus Christian dooty
>   This 'ere cuttin' folks's throats."

Is there any getting away from that for truth, however specious the arguments, in the beginning of the twentieth century any more than in the middle of the nineteenth ?

" John P. Robinson " is an immortal character, and there is no need to quote him here, but it is still worth while asking whether he was right, and whether our thought that " Christ went agin war an' pillage " *is* " an exploded idee." There are still some people, even among democrats, that have not scrapped the *Pious Editor's Creed*, and it would not harm us to re-read it and discover whether we accept it in fact if we repudiate it in expression.

> " In short, I firmly du believe
>   In Humbug generally,
> Fer it's a thing thet I perceive
>   To heve a solid vally ;
> This heth my faithful shepherd been,
>   In pasturs sweet heth led me,
> An' this'll keep the people green
>   To feed ez they have fed me."

The second series of the famous " Papers " dealt with the Civil War, and they have many lessons equally worth pondering, as thus :—

> " Wal, don't give up afore the ship goes down,
> It's a stiff gale, but Providence won't drown ;
> An 'God won't leave us yit to sink or swim,
> Ef we don't fail to du wut's right by Him."

or,

> " I jes' slip out o' sight
> An' take it out in a fair stan'-up fight
> With the one cuss I can't lay on the shelf,
> The crookedst stick in all the heap—
> > Myself."

And finally, as he seeks the vision of Peace, and decides he would rather take his chance to stand with the meanest slave at the bar of God than hold up there the dripping red hand of the warrior, he cries,

> " Come, while our country feels the lift
> > Of a gret instinct shoutin' ' Forwards ! '
> An' knows that freedom ain't a gift
> > That tarries long in han's o' cowards !
> Come, sech ez mothers prayed for, where
> > They kissed their cross with lips that quivered,
> An' bring fair wages for brave men,
> > A nation saved, a race delivered ! "

Might not these words have been written for this very hour ?

But in his other verse Lowell shows no less clearly his true democratic sympathies, and his belief in the spiritual principles that underly its powers. With this he identifies the very source of poetic inspiration.

> " A poet cannot strive for despotism ;
> His harp falls shattered, for it still must be
> The instinct of great spirits to be free."

The stirring *Stanzas on Freedom* and *The Fatherland* bear witness to the same faith.

The second verse from the former of these will be of interest to our women readers.

> " Women ! who shall one day bear
> Sons to breathe New England air,
> If ye hear without a blush,
> Deeds to make the roused blood rush
> Like red lava through your veins
> For your sisters now in chains,—
> Answer ! are ye fit to be
> Mothers of the brave and free ? "

Not less famous are his lines entitled *The Present Crisis*, with their stern trumpet-call.

> " Once to every man and nation comes the moment to decide,
> In the strife of Truth with Falsehood, for the good and evil side."

and closing with the splendid stanza :

> " New occasions teach new duties : Time makes ancient good uncouth,
> They must upward still, and onward, who would keep abreast of Truth :
> Lo ! before us gleam her camp-fires ! We ourselves must pilgrims be,
> Launch our Mayflower, and steer boldly through the desperate winter sea,
> Nor attempt the Future's portal with the Past's blood-rusted key."

It is significant of his sympathy with common people and common things that one of his loveliest poems is addressed to the dandelion.

> " How like a prodigal doth Nature seem,
> When thou, for all thy gold, so common art !
> Thou teachest me to deem
> More sacredly of every human heart."

Lowell's democracy was based on religious faith. There was no narrowness in his creed, but at heart it was the love of Christ that held him, and the interpretation of that divine brotherhood

breathes through such a poem as *The Vision of
Sir Launfal*, or in the lines to W. L. Garrison :

> " O Truth ! O Freedom ! how are ye still born
> In the rude stable, in the manger nurst !
> What humble hands unbar those gates of morn
> Through which the splendours of the New Day burst ! "

In the poem called *The Cathedral*, we have
something of the secret of his own religious life
revealed to us, as he shares his thoughts, awakened
by the Gothic miracle that is the glory of Chartres.
He tells us there how he knows :

> " Man cannot be God's outlaw if he would,"

and confesses how he has felt

> " That perfect disenthralment which is God."

These windows whisper to him of

> " The soul's east window of divine surprise."

Finally he announces his faith that the Cross,
that " bold type "

> " Of an unfinished life that sways the world,
> Shall tower as sovereign emblem over all."

---

* Lowell's complete works are published by Macmillan.

CHAPTER XI—
EDWARD CARPENTER.

THE greatest of Whitman's disciples is happily yet with us, living in his home near Sheffield, inspiring all who have the privilege of his personal friendship by his wonderful personality, and breathing new life and hope into countless other lives through the glowing pages of *Towards Democracy*. It would be interesting to know how many men and women hold that volume as one of their most priceless possessions. Some among our personal friends make it their constant companion and derive from it both vision and power for their work. This article will have more than fulfilled its purpose if it increases the number who turn to that well for refreshment and strength. Of all modern books of verse its appeal should be strongest to the majority in our Schools. It seems as if it were written for us, as if our laureate had been born for us in that son of nature, and large-hearted human soul— Edward Carpenter.

It does not detract from the originality of the book to admit that had *Leaves of Grass* never been written, we should probably have been without *Towards Democracy*. We have not begun to learn our lessons about literature until we have seen how new inspiration is born of the old. Chaucer derives from French Troubadours, whom most of us will never read. Shakespeare leans on old, forgotten plays, and translations of

EDWARD CARPENTER.

Photo: Alfred Mattison.

Greek and Latin authors; Tennyson's early poems are but echoes of his predecessors. Poets may be born, but they are not self-made. So when Carpenter found in Whitman his spiritual father, he does not lack originality in applying his methods, and reclothing his spirit to suit his own generation, and to render his verse the vehicle of a new and living world. He has himself told us the secret. " I have said in this brief note nothing about the influence of Whitman for the same reason that I have said nothing about the influences of the sun or the wind. These influences lie too far back and ramify too complexly to be traced. I met with William Rossetti's little selection from *Leaves of Grass* in 1868 or 1869, and read that and the original editions continuously for ten years. I never met with any other book (with the exception, perhaps, of Beethoven's sonatas) which I could read and re-read as I could this one. I find it difficult to imagine what my life would have been without it ; *Leaves of Grass* ' filtered and fibred ' my blood, but I do not think I ever tried to imitate it or its style. Against the inevitable drift out of the more classic forms of verse into a looser and freer rhythm I fairly fought, contesting the ground (' kicking against the pricks ') inch by inch during a period of seven years in numerous abortive and mongrel creations— till in 1881, I was finally compelled into the form (if such it can be called) of *Towards Democracy*."

This is a very illuminating statement. For Carpenter was a Cambridge man, trained in the discipline of her schools, and so had influences playing upon him that Whitman never felt, and yet the deliverance of his spirit brought with it the loosening of the shackles of form, and naturally produced the present vehicle of his song, with its strange and haunting beauty. He is a great artist in words, and we learn—the more we read him—to recognise the inward harmonies of his music.

At times—like Whitman—he writes in the more ordinary form of verse, and it is very beautiful. Let us take two illustrations :

> " Ah, surely to have known and to behold
>   The beauty that within the soul abides,
> For this Earth blossoms, and the skies unfold,
>   For this the Moon makes music in the tides ;
>
> " For this man rises from his mould of dust,
>   Ranges his life and looks upon the sun,
> For this he thrills and with adventurous trust
>   Forsakes this world and seeks a fairer one."

The second illustration is one of the most lovely lullabies in literature :

> " Croonie, croonie, baby, baby, up and down,
>   Sing song, all day long—
> Father's gone away for many a day, but he'll come back again,
>   Over the water before long.
>   *   *   *   *   *   *
> The great Earth shall be his cradle,
>   Rocking day by day ;
> Star-bespangled curtains spread
> Every night above his head ;
> Suns on suns shall gild his brow,
> Baby, baby, What art Thou ? "

Many are familiar with another example in the hymn sung so often, and never with greater fervour than in these days :

> " England arise ! the long, long night is over,
>   Faint in the East behold the dawn appear."

Carpenter began work as a curate under the inspiring influence of Maurice, from whom he doubtless drew much of that hope in the destinies of the people which has growingly possessed him. Then for years he was a University Extension Lecturer, thus touching our democracy sympathetically at another point. In 1881 he abandoned this work, and followed an overpowering impulse towards life in the open, and manual labour. He tells us that the open air is a necessity to him—he can feel the difference in merely passing through a doorway. " Always especially the sky seemed to contain for me the key, the inspiration ; the sight of it more than anything gave what I wanted (sometimes like a veritable lightning flash coming down from it on to my paper—I a mere witness, but agitated with strange transports)."

When the young men of Britain are learning more than ever before the love and fascination of an open-air life, surely this poet will speak in peculiarly appropriate language. Nothing has rejoiced the writer of these articles more than to learn they are appreciated in the trenches and camps where his friends are stationed. Carpenter

may bring to many of them an even wider horizon.
Hear him !

> " Sweet secret of the open air—
> That waits so long, and always there, unheeded.
>
> Something uncaught, so free, so calm, large, confident—
> The floating breeze, the far hills and broad sky,
> And every little bird and tiny fly or flower
> At home in the great Whole, nor feeling lost at all or forsaken,
> Sane man—slight man !
>
> And still the great world waits by the door as ever,
> The great world stretching endlessly on every hand, in deep on deep of
>   fathomless content—
> Where sing the morning stars in joy together,
> And all things are at home."

The great words round which his deepest songs
circle are Freedom, Democracy, Love. To this
man there are no closed doors. The universe is
athrob with God, for in Nature and in Man he
finds Him. Like Whitman, he greets even
death with a cheer, for is he not the great
Revealer ?

" Have you used the summer well, then the
winter shall be beautiful to you. Have you made
good use of Life, then Death shall be exceeding
glorious."

> " Thou canst not pass.
> I, too, am where thou art ; through all this life
> I walk the quiet kingdoms of the dead,
> Fast hand in hand with thee.
> Press now the sweet life of thy lips on mine ;
> I hold thee fast ;
> Not by the yellow sands nor the blue deep,
> But in my heart thy heart of hearts—
> A great star, growing, shining."

The word Democracy is indeed a great word, " turning the edges of the other words where they meet it," but we must be sure that we use it in the great sense in which this man uses it, if we are to make for it the same claim. It is far removed from the realm of politics, far even from the dreams of internationalism—it is a spirit and a power that makes humanity new. It is the inward idea and ideal of humanity—that which was and is in Him who called Himself the Son of Man.

> " See you not Me ? though I stand in the height of heaven,
> Glorious in all forms, am I become as nothing before you ?
> Though I walk through the streets with a basket on my arm, or leaning
> on a stick—or loiter in many disguises ?
> See you not Me ?
> Who have looked in your eyes so long for that glance of recognition ?
> Yet when you see me no form of maid or boy, or one mature or aged,
> Or the truth of anything shall escape you."

Surely here we have the prophet of Democracy, and it behoves us to learn patiently and slowly at his feet, till his thoughts sink into us and become our own.

The seer's gift has given him the power to interpret so many people. His poem on China, for example, breathes the spirit of that wonderful land far more truly than probably anything else in Western literature—certainly than anything of equal length. And so his pictures of Switzerland—see the fascinating *Tanzbödeli*. India, Sheffield, the marvel of the British Museum Library, all are there in these great pages.

With what exquisite beauty he touches the mystery of sex—how far more beautifully than Whitman, and yet with no less frankness. No finer example of this strain can be found than the little poem known as *The Babe* :

> " And then the Babe :
> A tiny perfect sea-shell on the shore
> By the waves gently laid (the awful waves !)—
> By trembling hands received—a folded message—
> A babe yet slumbering with a ripple on its face
> Remindful of the ocean.
> And two twined forms that overbend it, smiling,
> And wonder to what land Love must have journeyed,
> Who brought this back—this word of sweetest meaning ;
> *Two lives made one, and visible as one.*
> And herein all Creation."

To some readers of the volume the section to which most frequent return is made is that entitled *After Long Ages*. Here we have all the spiritual beauty and significance of Nature set before us in haunting phrases, that linger in our memory as does the sweetest music. The " sweet uses of Life " are all set before us, and the patience with which Nature calls again and again to our dull ears until we respond and share her joy.

> " O let not the flame die out !
> Cherished age after age in its dark caverns, in its holy temples cherished.
> Fed by pure ministers of love,
> Let not the flame die out ! "

The day of deliverance shall come to all : to the preacher, the prisoner, the sick, the artisan, " The coronet shall not be a hindrance to its wearer," " The railway porter shall open the carriage door and the long-expected friend shall descend to meet him," " The Magdalen shall run down to answer the knock at the door, and Jesus her lover Himself shall enter in." " Where the Master is there is Paradise."

How wonderful the vision of earth and its varied inhabitants he opens out before our eyes !

> " Spread O Earth, with blue lines of distant hills—stretch for the feet of men and all creatures !
>
> Sing, chant your hymns, O trees and winds and grass and immeasurable blue !
>
> Being transformed, being transformed into Thy likeness—Lord of heaven and earth !
>
> Being filled with love, having completed our pilgrimage,
> We also pass into peace and joy eternal."

We can quote no more but leave our readers to discover for themselves the jewels that are amply stored in that treasure-house. Here is a singer who weaves his songs from our every-day speech, their warp and woof is formed of our common experience, but the fabric is shot through and through with the silver threads of an interpretive imagination, and the pattern enriched with the golden shimmer of undying Love.*

---

* *Towards Democracy*, 3s. 6d., G. Allen and Son.

CHAPTER XII—JOHN MASEFIELD.

IN this chapter we consider the work of one of our younger contemporaries. He is essentially a poet of the twentieth century. He is young enough to be a member of our fighting forces, and has just issued a volume giving his experiences of the campaign in Gallipoli. He is, in the widest sense, a man of letters. He has edited several of our great classics, among them the travels of Marco Polo. He has written one of our best modern studies of Shakespeare, in the Home University Library. He is the author of one of the strongest and most hauntingly terrible of modern dramas—*Nan*, that holds us by its power as well as by its literary beauty, and two other prose plays we have from his pen. Nor must we forget his skill as a novelist—seen in *Captain Margaret*.

Here we have to deal with his poems. These —the greatest of them—have appeared in the pages of *The English Review*, and the blue-covered numbers that contain them are among the most precious possessions on our bookshelves.

This man is a lover of England and of the essential England—her sea, and her green fields. Like the first poet we treated in these studies— the author of *Piers the Ploughman*—the home of his heart seems to be that land near Malvern.

" Then hey for croft and hop-yard, and hill, and field and pond,
    With Bredon Hill before me, and Malvern Hill beyond."

For him the very name of Shropshire sings the melodies of joy.

> " That other day in Ercall when the stones
> Were unbleached white, like long unburied bones,
> While the bees droned and all the air was sweet
> From honey buried underneath my feet.
> Honey of purple heather and white clover
> Sealed in its gummy bags till summer's over."

and again in reference to the

> " Shropshire carters
> Born under Ercall where the white stones lie,
> Ercall that smells of honey in July."

Of the sea he sings with a deep love and a full knowledge, for he has sailed it in calm and in storms, and its unfailing call is upon him. In this he is a typical Englishman, and no one knows the "deep calling unto deep" better than he.

> " My road calls me, lures me,
> West, East, South and North.
> Most roads lead men homewards,
> My road leads me forth
> To add more miles to the tally
> Of grey miles left behind,
> In quest of that one beauty
> God put me here to find."

He knows the life of the workers, as his poem entitled *Biography* makes clear to us. It is no mere sympathetic insight, born of the imagination of poetic insight as with Crabbe or Wordsworth. He has had his

> " Days of labour also, loading, hauling ;
> Long days at winch or capstan, heaving, pawling ;
> The days with oxen, dragging stone from blasting,
> And dusty days in mills, and hot days masting.
> Trucking on dust-dry deckings smooth like ice,
> And hunts in mighty wool-racks after mice ;

> Days near the spring upon the sunburnt hill,
> Plying the maul or gripping tight the drill.
> Delights of work most real, delights that change
> The headache life of towns to rapture strange,
> Not known by townsmen nor imagined ; health
> That puts new glory upon mental wealth
> And makes the poor man rich."

Yet toil does not embitter this man, nor even poverty. Life has too great inherent riches to be dependent on outward things. That is why his verse affords so healthy and constant a tonic. The poem we have just quoted concludes with four lines that cannot be too deeply impressed on our minds, or too frequently recalled in difficult days.

> " Best trust the happy moments.   What they gave
> Makes men less fearful of the certain grave,
> And gives his work compassion and new eyes,
> The days that made us happy make us wise."

And again he has given us the same message in one of his early poems.

> " Laugh and be merry, remember, better the world with a song,
> Laugh and be proud to belong to the old proud pageant of man.
> Laugh and be merry together like brothers akin,
> Guesting awhile in the rooms of a beautiful inn."

Yet this is no easy optimism. Tragedy lies at the back of all his greater poems. These same " daffodil fields " of which he writes are the background of sorrow, shame, and sin, and he sometimes seems to revel too much in the ugly facts of life, and in its sordid shadows.

It would be so, were he a pessimist ; but he is not, for love is supreme in his universe, and

there is a goal which even these tired feet of men
will one day reach.

He sings of it in his verses on Sir Bors and his
quest of the Holy Grail. He is worn out, weary,
seated on a shrunk and tottering steed.

> " It will happen at last, as my horse limps down the fell,
> A star will glow like a note God strikes on a silver bell,
> And the bright white birds of God will carry my soul to Christ,
> And the sight of the Rose, the Rose, will pay for the years of hell."

And in another poem in the same volume—

> " Friends and lovers we have none, nor wealth nor blest abode,
> But the hope of the City of God at the other end of the road."

And in his poem *August*, 1914, written on the
outbreak of war there is a mystic expression of
the same truth in the terrible sacrifice of those
who

> " Sadly rose and left the well-loved Downs
> And so by ship to sea, and knew no more
> The fields of home, the byres, the market towns,
> Nor the dear outline of the English shore.
> But knew the misery of the soaking trench,
> The freezing in the rigging, the despair
> In the revolting sound of the wrench
> When the blind soul is flung upon the air,
> And died (uncouthly most) in foreign lands
> For some idea but dimly understood
> Of an English city never built by hands,
> Which love of England prompted and made good."

The longer and best known poems—in order of
their publication are *The Everlasting Mercy*,
The Widow in the Bye Street, *Dauber*, and *The
Daffodil Fields*. As each tells a story they are
difficult to quote from in a short paper, and they
must be read and studied to get their full beauty

and meaning. They are all alive with passages
of the most marvellous loveliness in description of sea and land. Seldom, if ever, has the
witchery of the sea been put before us in verse
with the fascination of the pictures in *Dauber*—
the strange creature who essayed to paint
something of the glory that his eyes saw
and his heart conceived. This character has a
curious parallel in J. C. Snaith's recent novel, *The
Sailor*, where the same grip of the sea is felt by
a soul, who only long afterwards is able to produce
it in literary form. What can be finer than this
description of the ship's arrival at some foreign
port ?

> " To come, after long months, at rosy dawn,
>   Into the placid blue of some great bay,
> Treading the quiet water like a fawn,
>   Ere yet the morning haze was blown away,
>   A rose-flushed figure putting aside the grey,
> And anchoring there before the city smoke
> Rose, or the church bells rang, or men awoke.
>
> " There in the sunset's flush they went aloft
>   And unbent sails in that most lovely hour,
> When the light gentles and the wind is soft,
>   And beauty in the heart breaks like a flower."

But it is the wonderful soul-stories that haunt
us. They are all about very common people—
the roughest and the poorest, but they are
" human documents " with a vengeance. The
narrative of the sailor-artist, his home struggles
—the mockery of his mates—his tragic death
when he felt victory was all but his—pulls at
our heart strings. The pathetic figure of the

widow with her prodigal son, and all her endeavour—warm with a mother's love—to keep him straight. Then his execution, and her return to the lovely house with dreams of the past.

> " We made this room so snug,
> He sat beside me in his little chair,
> I gave him real tea sometimes in his mug
> He liked the velvet in the patchwork rug,
> He used to stroke it, did my pretty son,
> He called it Bunny, little Jimmy done."

It is genius that makes poetry out of such simple elements. Never since Bunyan has such a thing been written in English as *The Everlasting Mercy*—the story of the conversion of the village scapegrace, with its wonderful pictures of the man himself—the old mother afraid of his influence on her lad, and of the courageous Quaker lady, who were the two human factors in his salvation. The scene at the bar of the public houses is unforgettable, and then the man going out into the darkness, but finding a wonderful light there, for " he had done with sin."

> " I knew that Christ had given me birth
> To brother all the souls on earth."

It is full of the real deep joy of the mystery of God's love in the human soul, and should be an ever-welcome message in our schools.

One of Masefield's latest tasks has been in his play, *Good Friday*, to re-tell for us the story of the Crucifixion. It is beautifully done, the awfulness of the tragedy in its varied effect upon

the lives of the main figures in the dread tragedy—
Pilate, his wife, Herod, the Roman Centurion,
and the Jewish people has great elements of
power. The original feature is the introduction
of a poor-half-witted blind man, who alone sees
the real significance of the deeds of the day.
This is very true in the poet's method. It is the
heart of humanity—even at its lowest and least
lovely level that may often enter into the secrets
of the highest for to these humblest of His
brethren Christ opens the door. We shall close
with this madman's song, which forms also the
last message of the play.

> " I cannot see what others see,
>   Wisdom alone is kind to me,
>   Wisdom that comes from agony.
>
> " Wisdom that lives in the pure skies,
>   The untouched star, the spirit's eyes ;
>   O Beauty, touch me, make me wise." *

* Masefield's Poems are issued in separate volumes at 3s. 6d. each, but the
best can be found in numbers of the *English Review*, 1s. each.

CHAPTER XIII—
WILFRID WILSON GIBSON.

THE discovery of a new poet is to all lovers of literature one of the purest and most satisfactory of pleasures, and when one first came upon some of the poems of this clear-visioned and gifted singer of our own day, we knew that a man with his own message, and his peculiarly personal genius for its delivery had arisen in our midst. We believe he is a Northener a native like our first English poet, of Northumbria. He is still a young man, so our hopes of future fulfilment (not belied by his latest work) are well justified. He is evidently progressing, and we earnestly trust he will be one of the most potent voices of the new democracy, cleansed, quickened, strengthened by the present strife.

In the pages of various journals and magazines in the early years of this century appeared various short poems from the pen of W. W. Gibson, and in 1903, Elkin Mathews published in his " Vigo Cabinet " a little volume entitled *Urlyn the Harper*, followed almost immediately by *The Queen's Vigil*.

The titles suggest the subjects and the manner of mediæval romance. The poet found his inspiration, where so many found it before him, in legends similar to those of the court of King Arthur. Here is one example :—

> " I sang of lovers, and she praised my song,
> The while the king looked on her with cold eyes,
> And twixt them on the throne sat mailèd-wrong.

> I sang of Lancelot and of Guinevere,
>   While in her face I saw old sorrows rise,
> And throned between them cowered naked Fear.
>
> I sang of Tristram and La Belle Isoud,
>   And how they fled the anger of King Mark
> To live and love deep sheltered in a wood.
>
> Then, bending low, she spake, sad-voiced and sweet,
>   The while grey terror crouched between them stark,
> ' Sing now of Aucassin and Nicolete.' "

There is much in such verse of lingering love-liness, and artistic skill, but little to give promise of new power, and of a poet fathoming the depths of modern needs, and bringing sunshine to sad places. He shows in these verses a marvellous sense of music, and of the subtle possibilities of verse manipulation. In this first volume there is a series of short poems, called *Faring South*, which points the new direction in which his mind was already turning, for they deal with the common people. They are charming little cameos, clear-cut as a Greek gem, allusive and haunting as a Japanese lyric. They sketch the toilers, mowers, goat-herds, stone-breakers, washer-women, shepherds. Here is one :—

> " Beneath the droop of willows tall and lithe
> The mower moves with circle-sweeping scythe,
> Mid hollow-snapping rushes, severed clean,
> Which fall in outward raying spears of green.
>
> His swaying body and the flashing blade
> Swing on in rhythmic ease from shade to shade,
> Unstayed, unswerving, slaying without strife,
> One chant of doubtless Life and Death in Life."

Another element of the Middle Ages is prominent in some of these poems, namely, the religious one, and nowhere is it more exquisitely expressed than in the poem called *The Eternal Way*, which shows that the significance of the tragedy of the Cross has penetrated the heart of this poet, and prepared the way for that sympathetic treatment of human sorrow that we find in his later work.

His next volume, *The Golden Helm*, revealed his power to write good blank verse, and to make it the medium of a moving tale, and this marks another step of progress towards his goal. Other poems in the same volume are written in dialogue form, an indication that he is finding his way to the proper forms for the expression of his individual genius. *The Vision*, a Christmas mystery—shows remarkable originality, and its strange theme is returned to with much greater power in *The Queen's Crags*, a poem in *Borderlands* (1914). In *The Nets of Love* (1905) we have much lovely work, but nothing finer or more significant than *The Lambing*, the story of a shepherd who is forced to leave his wife, with her new-born babe, that he may go to the aid of his ewes. On his return, he finds the mother dead, but the touch of the little babe's hands upon his cheek, reveals the fact

> " That not for me yet was there rest from love and strife,
> I caught the babe to my breast and looked in the eyes of life."

In 1907 he applied newly discovered poetic

forms to dialogue and to the lives of the English working classes, and we get from his pen *Stone folds* and *On the Threshold*, full of fine achievement but richer still in promise. They consist of tales of the shepherds and farm folk of the fells and are full of beauty and pathos. In writing them he must have found that he had accomplished deliverance, for his dedicatory poem contains these lines :—

> " But as once more I watch the stars
>   Rekindle in the glittering West,
> Beyond the fell tops' naked scars
>   Life rouses in me with new zest.
>
> The immortal wakens in my blood,
>   Beneath the wind's relentless thresh,
> And universal life at flood
>   Breaks through the bonds of bone and flesh."

In 1910, was published *Akra the Slave*, but in his preface to the poem he tells us it was written six years earlier, therefore about the same time as the poems we have just been considering. It is an experiment in verse, and in spite of what some critics have said, a justifiable experiment. Its medium is modified and very irregular blank verse, but the art is extremely subtle ; its pauses, swift passionate rushes, and alliterative music is a sheer joy. The story is a simple one, told with wonderful power, and did space permit one would like to dwell on its many beauties. Its importance for us, however, lies in the proof that the new medium had been discovered for his new message, and this came in 1908, in the volume,

Daily Bread, which I have no hesitation in saying is one of the most remarkable books of recent years. The poet himself tells us he had sought for some simpler form of speech, that would be nearer the language of those he desired to delineate and he has found it. The inspiration is drawn from the heart of the working-classes, their joys and sorrows. A careful and frequent reading of these poems will do more to open some people's eyes to the problems that press upon us than will reams of government reports.

All classes of toilers are here brought before us, and we are shown the secrets of their lives—fisher-folk, agricultural labourers, miners, iron-workers, railwaymen, and the weary strugglers for work, who cannot find it, and whose children die of sheer starvation. William James's moral equivalent of war is here. These men and women are all heroes and heroines. Someone has compared Gibson's poetry to the pictures of François Millet, and the comparison is a just one. As Henry Drummond used to say of the *Angelus*, it contains the three great realities, work, love and religion. So do these wonderful poems. They cannot be represented in extracts, they must be read in their entirety, and so we must see their meaning for ourselves. There could be no better subject for First Half-hours in our schools than a series of these carefully read by groups of men and women. Better still if they were learned and recited so that their dramatic power might be felt. Some of us might, for the first time, realise the magic and power of poetry by this means. Here we have, as Gibson himself says

> " The restless deeps that, day and night,
> Surge with the life-song of humanity."

It is quite certain that those who make their first acquaintance with *The Garret*, *The Night Shift*, *Mates*, and *Summer Dawn* will have found in the poet a new friend.

In some ways the next series of volumes, published in 1912, entitled *Fires*, were more remarkable, for here he made living poems of such elements as hardly seemed possible. *The Shop* is a great triumph. A little shop in a back street, the regular customer, an artisan, the shopkeeper full of anxiety for his sick child, and of memories of his own boyhood's days, in Cornwall where

> " 'Twould be primroses, blowing everywhere,
> Primroses, and primroses and primroses   .   .   .
> You'd never know what primroses were,
> Unless you'd seen them growing in the West."

How the haunting words gave new music to the workman at his anvil, and then the boy's chance of recovery in the Cornish air, and his return well and strong, much more enamoured of pigs than of primroses !

Later volumes are *Thoroughfares* and *Border-lands*, with fuller evidence of his power in dialogue verse, and one sad little play called *Womenkind*.

Since the war, we have two volumes, one called
Battle, and the other *Friends*. Many of the
battle poems are very terrible, but they bring
home to us the true pathos of war, and some of
them reveal, very poignantly, the secret agony
of waiting hearts at home.

> " He went, and he was gay to go,
>   And I smiled on him as he went.
> My boy ! 'twas well he couldn't know
>   My darkest dread, or what it meant,—
> Just what it meant to smile and smile
>   And let my son go cheerily—
> My son   .   .   .   and wondering all the while
>   What stranger would come back to me."

In *Friends* there are some lovely memorial
verses to his brother-poet, Rupert Brooke, but
in two cases he returns to his love of the workers
—in the haunting sonnet *Gold*, with its parable of
the goldbeater, and the *Ice-cart*, showing how
common things can awake poetic visions.

Beautiful poems of wedded love close the
book, and one of these—perfect in its beauty—
must be my last quotation :

> " Red roses floating in a crystal bowl
> You bring, O Love ; and in your eyes I see
> Blossom on blossom, your warm love of me
> Burning within the crystal of your soul—
> Red roses floating in a crystal bowl."

In his last volume (*Livelihood*) Gibson has
returned to his earlier method, and has given us a
series of monologues uttered, in the main, by
working folk in moments of stress and crisis in
their lives. It may be a collier lost in an old

mine, or an ironworker with his father lying dead at home. Or he may picture for us the soldier in No-man's-land between the trenches, or a doctor fighting stern battles with death. The mother, picking strawberries, learns how her mechanical task deadens the fever of anxiety for the absent loved one, or the boy, fresh from school, feels the call of the land bid him take up the ancestral service on the land. In lighter mood we join with the worker in holiday hours, but everywhere we learn one of the secrets of life's sweetness and sorrow in the common things of life, with its material for comedy and tragedy.

(Most of Gibson's Poems are published by Elkin Mathews at 1s. a volume.

GEORGE MEREDITH.
Photo: Frederick Hollyer.

CHAPTER XIV—
GEORGE MEREDITH.

TO every ten readers of modern English who know George Meredith as a novelist there is probably only one who knows and loves him as a poet. Yet the bulk of the poetry he has written is considerable, as the volume of his collected poems, published by Messrs. Constable in 1912, proves. It runs to 578 pages, and there are few modern books of poetry that so well repay our study as does this one. The majority of readers will find enough for a start in the small volume of Selected Poems, but whichever is chosen and opened for the first time contains a rich feast.

He is not an easy writer either in verse or prose, being only equalled in obscurity by Browning. The difficulty in both poets springs from the same causes—the richness and intensity of the thought, and the curiously condensed style, increased by the unfamiliar nature of the metaphors and their rapid change, often suggesting more than they express. It is not that the words are difficult—they are often very short and simple, but their abruptness and the amount that is left to the reader's mind to interpret makes the reading hard. Take the following lines from *Hard Weather* as an example :

> " Is the land ship ? we are rolled, we drive
> Tritonly, cleaving hiss and hum ;
> Whirl with the dead, or mount or dive,
> Or down in dregs, or on in scum.

> And drums the distant, pipes the near,
> And vale and hill are grey in grey,
> As when the surge is crumbling sheer,
> And sea-mews wing the haze of spray.
> Clouds—are they bony-witches ?—swarms,
> Darting swift on the robber's flight,
> Hurry an infant sky in arms :
> It peeps, it becks ; 't is day, 't is night.
> Black while over the loop of blue
> The swathe is closed, like shroud on corse.
> Lo, as if swift the Furies flew,
> The Fates at heel at a cry to horse ! "

The majority of the words are of one syllable, and the grammar is clear enough, and yet most readers will find they have to read the lines more than once before the idea they convey becomes clear.

Of many of his most famous and beautiful poems this is not the place to speak, for it is only with one message of his poetry that we have here to deal. Yet mention must be made of one of the most charming love poems in our language, *Love in the Valley*. It must have been a great favourite with its author, for we have two versions of it, one written in 1851, when he was twenty-three years of age, and the second twenty-seven years later. Thus the man of middle life set his seal to the true vision of love seen in his youth, a sure token that experience had for him verified imagination.

Of the only stanza of the poem I have space to quote, Robert Louis Stevenson wrote : " It haunted me and made me drunk like wine."

> " When her mother tends her before the laughing mirror,
> Tying up her laces, looping up her hair,
> Often she thinks, were this wild thing wedded,
> More love should I have, and much less care.
>
> When her mother tends her before the lighted mirror,
> Loosening her laces, combing down her curls,
> Often she thinks were this wild thing wedded,
> I should miss but one for many boys and girls."

The most illuminating critic of Meredith's poetry has said that other two lines of this poem may well be classed among the greatest lines in English. They occur in a verse descriptive of the dawn on a day before the lover has learned from his beloved the secret of her love.

> " Maiden still the morn is ; and strange she is, and secret :
> Strange her eyes ; her cheeks are cold as cold sea-shells."

We must leave our readers to discover the strange tragedy of *Modern Love*, told in a series of stanzas, some of which stand comparison with the finest poetry in our language. It is a sad story, but intensely vital, telling

> " How silence best can speak
> The awful things when Pity pleads for Sin."

Without our guidance they must wander through the mystic *Woods of Westermain*, and study the *Ballads and Poems of Tragic Life*, for we must now turn to the poems that mainly concern our immediate purpose.

In his novels Meredith has given some wonderful pictures of the English rustic, with his shrewd philosophy of life, and his quaint humour. In the poems we find the same traits as in the narrative poem *Grandfather Bridgeman*, or more strikingly still in *Juggling Jerry*—where the picture of the old man who has made his living by amusing and fooling the crowd, and now lies dying in his old wife's arms is full of these mingled chords :

> " Yes, my old girl ! and it's no use crying :
>   Juggler, constable, king, must bow ;
> One that outjuggles all's been spying
>   Long to have me, and he has me now.
>
> Lean me more up the mound ; now I feel it :
>   All the old heath-smells ! Ain't it strange ?
> There's the world laughing, as if to conceal it,
>   But He's by us, juggling the change."

In *Martin's Puzzle* we have a very modern setting of the world-old problems of Job. The village philosopher is puzzled at the thought of a tender, loving, gracious girl, crippled and tortured by man's thoughtlessness and brutality. Can there be a law or a God of Love behind a universe, where such things are permitted ? Can it be that these things are permitted in order to teach us lessons ?

> " It's a roundabout way, with respect let me add,
>   If Molly goes crippled that we may be taught."

Then the thought comes to him that perhaps he is judging all things from a single false note, which though it sounds discordant, may be part of the great harmony.

> " Is the Universe one immense Organ, that rolls
>   From devils to angels ?   I'm blind with the sight.
> It pours such a splendour on heaps of poor souls !
>   I might try at kneeling with Molly to-night.''

In *The Patriot Engineer* and *The Beggar's Soliloquy* we have examples of the more purely humorous side, as also in *The Old Chartist*, on which we may linger for a moment. He is an old man who has just returned from transportation for his views, but who, in spite of her injustice to him, loves old England still.

> " Whate'er I be, old England is my dam ! "

He wanders among the old scenes on this summer morning, and stands by the little stream that runs out of His Grace's park :

> " My lord can't lock the water ; nor the lark,
>   Unless he kills him, can my lord keep down.
>   Up, is the song-note.
>   I've tried it too :—for comfort and renown,
>   I rather pitch'd upon the wrong note.''

Then he sights an old brown water-rat at his careful toilet, and moralises in a quaint fashion upon the proceeding. He comes into a saner view of life during the process, and has kinder views of everyone.

> " In my life
> I never found so true a democrat.
>   Base occupation
> Can't rob you of your own esteem, old rat !
>   I'll preach you to the British nation.''

Meredith was himself a great lover of England, but by no means a blind lover. He was intensely

patriotic, but critical in his patriotism.   He could
sing in praise of Nelson a rousing ballad, one of
the finest of its kind we possess, with its splendid
refrain :

> " He leads ; we hear our Seaman's call
>   In the roll of battles won ;
> For he is Britain's Admiral
>   Till setting of her sun,"

but he had no love of wild Imperialism.   He gave
strong warning against

> " This little Isle's insatiable greed
> For continents."

He saw error in both sides in the Boer war, and
wrote of it frankly, as

> " Of man's descent insane
> To brute."

His ideal for his country was

> " That in the Britain thus endowed,
> Imperial means beneficent,
> And strength to service vowed."

We cannot help wishing he had been alive
to give us much needed counsel in these days.

His Celtic temperament enabled him to sym-
pathise with and interpret the ideals of Ireland
and of France.   From his poem on Ireland how
wise are these words :

> " A nation she, and formed to charm,
>   With heart for heart and hands all round.
> No longer England's broken arm,
>   Would England know where strength is found.

> And strength to-day is England's need ;
> To-morrow it may be for both
> Salvation : heed the portents, heed
> The warnings ; free the mind from sloth."

Written in 1909, how prophetic these words sound, and one is struck with the same note of wonderful prevision in the poems on France. One was written in 1871, and the others in 1898, but they contain many passages that might have been written to-day, and show a rare insight into our neighbours' spiritual character. We can only quote these few lines :

> " Soaring France !
> Now is Humanity on trial in thee :
> Now mayest thou gather human kind in fee ;
> Now prove that Reason is a quenchless scroll,
> Make of calamity thine aureole,
> And bleeding, lead us thro' the troubles of the sea."

Of Russia, he sums up the situation in a word in his poem *The Crisis :*

> " A soul : that art thou."

while his sympathy with Italy's struggle for unity and freedom are seen in his poem on *The Cen-tenary of Garibaldi*, and he sings in his novel *Vittoria*, where he paraphrases Mazzini's message,

> " Our life is but a little holding, but
> To do a mighty labour ; we are one
> With heaven and the stars when it is spent
> To serve God's arm ; else die we with the Sun."

There is no space in this article to deal with the fascinating subject of Meredith's philosophy of Life, and with what he calls the " Reading of

Earth." His forms of teaching the great truths are not the usual forms, but fundamentally he believed as the best men ever must that the real strength of life consists in spiritual communion and fellowship, in the truest brotherhood, in education, and in prayer.

Writing of England he cries :

> " Has she ears to take forewarnings,
> She will cleanse her of her stains,
> Feed and speed for braver mornings,
> Valorously the growth of grains ? "

If men were sane enough to learn these lessons well, and to seek the highest he has no fear for the future.   Earth

> " Has wonders in looms,
> Revelations, delights.   I can hear a faint crow
> Of the cock of fresh mornings, far, far, yet distant."

> " If courage should falter 'tis wholesome to kneel.
> Remember that well, for the secret with some,
> Who pray for no gift, bur have cleansing in prayer,
> And free from impurities tower-like stand."

He is a firm believer in evolutionary progress in all directions, and therefore one of our primary duties is provision for future generations.

> " Keep the young generations in hail,
> And bequeath them no tumbled house ! "

Of his study of human progress a very interesting example is to be found in the poem entitled *Forest History*, round an exposition and illustration of which I can imagine many of our Schools having a most delightful and profitable first half-hour !

If my readers will turn to Meredith's poetry they will discover not only new sources of joy, but fresh ideas of life and conduct, and much mental stimulus and moral tonic. They will find that he has fought his battles bravely, and come out triumphant through his faith in man and his destiny. Probably one of these favourite poems will prove to be *The Thrush in February*, and with some of its haunting and inspiring lines I must leave them to discover for themselves fresh treasures.

> " Those warriors of the fighting brain,
> Give worn Humanity new youth.
>   This they knew :
> That life begets with fair increase
> Beyond the flesh, if life be true.
>
> Full lasting is the song, though he,
> The singer, passes : lasting too,
> For souls not lent in usury,
> The rapture of the forward view." *

---

* George Meredith's complete Poems are issued in one volume, at 7s. 6d., but there is also a good volume of *Selected Poems*, published by Constable at 1s.

CHAPTER XV—
SIR RABINDRANATH TAGORE

FOR the next poet of the present series we turn to that great land, which forms part of this mighty Empire—the land of India. Its people are united to us by ties of race, and their ancient language lies at the roots of our own. When we were as yet barbarians, their civilisation was hoary, and their religion venerable. In recent years there has been a renascence of art and literature, and no name is more highly honoured among the people than that of Ravindranatha Thakkur, whom we in England know by the name of Rabindranath Tagore.

He belongs to an ancient and honourable family in Bengal, and his father was famous as a philosopher and a saint. He belonged to one of the recent religious sects of India somewhat akin to the Unitarians among ourselves, and his religious addresses are full of beauty and power. He was much given to the practice of religious meditation, and he built a house and surrounded it with grounds, where all were welcome who desired quiet opportunities for spiritual thought and worship.

The sons of the house are all famous as philosophers, poets, artists, and in other capacities. The poet with whom we have here to deal was born in 1861, at Calcutta, and early in life lost his mother. His childhood was very lonely, and in many ways unhappy. He was not like other

SIR RABINDRANATH TAGORE.

Photo: Bourne & Shepherd.

boys, and at school his teachers did not understand him, and were often not only unsympa-
thetic but cruel. When his father learned the
true state of affairs, he provided private tutors
for his son, who soon showed his aptitude for
study, and quite early revealed poetic gifts, and
before he was eighteen his work showed ample
promise.

About that age he paid his first visit to England
with the intention of studying law. The subject
proved uncongenial, and he returned to India to
take charge of his father's estate. In this capacity
he found himself and his two great teachers—
nature and the common people. Nature, as he
tells us, was his loving companion, and seemed
to play with him the game of hiding something always in her hand for him to discover,
and so great was the wonder of the search that
nothing seemed impossible.

With his father's workpeople he entered into
intimate relations, and so became the revealer of
their inner spirit. His marriage—an ideally
happy one—took place when he was about
twenty-three, and as children came to his home
he found new teachers. Nowhere unless it be
in the poems of R. L. Stevenson, do we find life
so beautifully set forth as in that charming
volume *The Crescent Moon*. The eternal mystery
and beauty of the mother and her child are sung
with fascinating sweetness, and the child's dreams
and fancies told in haunting verse. How lovely,

for example, is the poem called *Vocation*, where the child would choose to be a hawker, for his freedom, a gardener, since he may dig when and where he will, and no one chides him for being muddy and wet, and lastly the night watchman, since he need never go to bed !

Humorous and tender is the mother's address to her child whom others chide for little faults, concluding with the lines :

> " Everybody knows how you love sweet things,—is that why they call
> you greedy ?
> O fie ! What then would they call us who love you ? "

The English form of his verse is not a translation, but a version made by himself. Of course it does not rhyme, but its measure and cadence is very lovely. In order to gain a proper conception of the beauty of his work it is necessary to hear some native of the land chant the original verses, or sing them to the melodies the poet has himself composed. The charm and exquisite music is then revealed.

The world of childhood taught him deep truths. It was to him a realm " where Reason makes kites of her laws and flies them, and Truth sets Facts free from its fetters." Perhaps most beautiful of all his child poems is one of which I quote two verses, for it shows how he links this feeling of parentage on to the mystic interpretation of the universe, and how he feels that the effort to enter into the child's soul

brings him close to the secret of the Supreme
Spirit.

> " When I sing to make you dance, I truly know why there is music in
> leaves, and why waves send their chorus of voices to the heart of
> the listening earth—.
> " When I sing to make you dance.
> " When I kiss your face to make you smile, my darling, I surely
> understand what the pleasure is that streams from the sky in
> morning light, and what delight that is which the summer breeze
> brings to my body—
> When I kiss you to make you smile."

When he was about thirty-five years of age he
lost by death his wife, the beloved daughter that
seemed to take her place, and his son. But in this
terrible fire of affliction his soul only gained
strength, and his spiritual vision became all the
more keen. In finding comfort for himself he
discovered its secret to others, and the poems that
date from this period are among the finest he
has written. Here is his confession :

> " It is this overspreading pain that deepens with loves and desires into
> sufferings and joys in human homes, and this it is that ever melts
> and flows in songs through my poet's heart."

But very wisely he found another fruit on this
bitter tree—the fruit of service. In 1901, he
turned the religious retreat his father had prepared—with its lovely native name meaning
" The Abode of Peace,"—into a school for boys.
He modelled it on Indian lines, though he
brought to its development all he had learned
in the educational institutions of the west. It

was to be a new kind of *Asram* or forest school, and all who have visited it tell us how well the scheme has been carried out. Beginning with but two or three boys the school has now almost two hundred pupils. In the early morning the visitor is awakened by singing as the boys' choir goes round the grounds. Household work, physical exercise, a quarter of an hour's meditation and a religious service all precede regular lessons, which are held from 8 to 11.30. The afternoon is filled with lighter work and recreation, and in the evenings further study—story-telling, amusements, and finally songs conclude the day at 9.30. The elder boys teach in the neighbouring villages, thus learning all the while to impart to others what they have learned. The school is managed by committees of the boys themselves—a fresh captain being chosen for each week, and all cases of discipline are decided by their own court.

It is a beautiful and interesting experiment, and we await with keen expectation its further development. Mr. Ramsay Macdonald wrote an account of his visit to the school and is full of praise of its open-air life and its beautiful freedom, where " everything," he says, " is peaceful, natural and happy." The poet himself is the inspiration of the whole place, and when he talks or teaches the boys love to sit at his feet.

" I read Rabindranath every day ; to read one

line of his is to forget all the troubles of the world," said an Indian gentleman to Mr. W. B. Yeats. This is a great and striking tribute to his power, and we rejoice in nothing more than in the fact that he exercises his gift for the benefit of all. It is the true spirit of democracy that we find in his pages, for it is of man as man that he writes. As one of his Indian interpreters has said, "His heroes and heroines are drawn from the ordinary people, and their simple joys and sorrows are rendered for us in musical language with extraordinary insight and depth of emotion." Perhaps the most perfect illustration the English reader can find of this statement is in his little play, *The Post Office*.

We have not reached the highest message Tagore has for us till we speak of his mystic consciousness of God. This fills all his religious verse as its very centre and motive. Yet it is perfectly simple and natural, and we feel that he is giving us the insight because he means us to share it.

> "Entering into my heart unbidden as one of the common crowd, unknown to me, my king, thou didst press the signet of eternity upon many a fleeting moment."

Yet we are not to become ascetics. Those who seek to serve God thus are mistaken. Nothing must hedge us off from what he somewhere terms "the great fair of common human life." God is to be found :

> " Where the tiller is tilling the hard ground, and where the path-maker
>   is breaking stones.
> He is with them in sun and in shower, and His garment is covered with
>   dust . . .
>   . . . What harm is there if thy clothes become tattered and
>   stained ?
> Meet Him and stand by Him in toil and in sweat of thy brow."

That unseen Friend is always with us, His " silent steps " haunt the recesses of our soul, and " the golden touch of His feet " brings our meed of joy.

The secret of all this gladness and power is revealed in a prayer contained in one of his poems, which reminds us of the famous couplet in *In Memoriam :*

> " Our wills are ours we know not how,
>   Our wills are ours to make them Thine."

The Indian poet cries :

> " Give me the strength to surrender my strength to Thy will with love."

There can be no more hopeful outlook for the democracy of India than that it should follow this great guide raised up among its own people, and surely we should be thankful that such a voice has spoken to us also, and that our study of these poets of the democracy includes one who has seen in the little child the image of the Divine and the heir of the spiritual kingdom, for therein lies the hope of the new humanity and the promise of the future.

[NOTE : Tagore's works are unfortunately expensive, but we must remember he applies all his profits, as he did also the large sum of the Nobel Prize, to his school. If we buy one of his books, therefore, we are helping his work. An excellent little study in the series " Biographies of Eminent Indians," is published on the poet and his work by Messrs. Nateson & Co., Madras, at 4 annas (4d.). This can be obtained in England.]

CHAPTER XVI—
COLONIAL DEMOCRATIC POETS.

THERE is at least one good effect of the great war, and that we hope will be a lasting one, it has brought us into closer and more intimate touch with our colonies. Contrary to the expectation of our enemies, and probably of all the onlooking nations, the bonds that link us have been forged more firmly, and the days to come will see us in more vital and effective union than we have ever been in the past. The presence of so many colonials in our midst has helped us to understand them, and to learn at first hand their point of view. It will be a great gain if their literature also becomes better known here, for one has met many people in the past, with considerable claims to education, who have asked in the most surprised way, "What, have the colonies got poets of their own?"

It need not astound us if the democratic spirit is pretty clear in the verses that come from these lands, and if the majority of the poets find themselves not only close to nature in its wildest and most primitive aspects, but also dealing with man in his elemental moods—some of them we shall also find have attempted not unsuccessfully, to interpret for us the men of other races with whom they have become close neighbours. The reading of Colonial poetry will be the best way in which many of us will learn to understand the men and women of these lands, which we shall never be able to visit, but to which more and more of our boys and girls will find their way in the days that are not far off.

Probably the earliest of Colonial poets to find recognition in Histories of English Literature is Thomas Pringle, a Scotsman, who sailed to Cape Town in 1820, where he remained for six years, and wrote poems and other works on the Colony. His poem beginning :

> " Afar in the desert I love to ride,
> With the silent Bush-boy alone by my side,"

received extremely warm praise from Coleridge, who reckoned it one of the finest lyrics in the language. It is full of the sense of the beauty and wonder of the vast solitudes, whence comes a voice,

> " Which banishes bitterness, wrath and fear,
> Saying, ' Man is distant, but God is near.' "

His experiences abroad made him a zealous supporter of the anti-slavery movement, and one of his poems tells the touching story of a Bechuana boy adopted by himself and his wife, who

> " With woman's gentle art
> Unlocked the fountains of his heart."

The union of the races in South Africa has been finely described in a poem by Watermeyer, the burden of which is contained in the lines :

> " English are you ? or Dutch ?
> Both, neither. How ?
> The land I dwell in Dutch and English plough."

Of recent South African poets C. Gouldsbury is the most suggestive and characteristic. In his pages we catch the various moods of that life in the lovely land of the magic plains.

> " Tapestries of tender green,
>   Screens of grass like cloth of gold,
> Bits of bushland in between,
>   Where the pinky buds unfold.
>   Wisps of smoke from heathen fires
>   On the Plain of our Desires."

The poignant sorrows are dealt with also—the man who sees the cottage he had reared with such care burned to the ground, and with its loss his hopes for the future perish—the parting with children and his wife, because the conditions of life demand it, and the noble heroism of the women—

> " They serve you in silence gaily,
>   Whole-hearted and serene,
> Watching their youth die daily
>   Into the Might-have-been.
> Scouring the seas between,
>   To share their husbands' place,
> Your women of the outposts
>   Are the Mothers of the Race."

Once and again he turns also to the native peoples, and, with wonderful success, penetrates into their minds, and sets forth in telling verse their view of life. Here, perhaps, his real service to the cause of democracy is most apparent, for he reveals to us the same problems and sufferings that beset our own souls finding their echo in those of our coloured brethren. Take these lines from a song of the native bearers on the track :

> " My brothers, the dawn is grey,
> And the legs are stiff, and the arms are sore,
> So hitch the load on your backs once more,
> There's many a blazing mile in store,
>   For you've got to travel to-day ! "

And with fatalistic calmness they face the dreary outlook :

> " The gods have settled the business thus,
>   It's nothing to do with the likes of us."

These colonials have much cheery philosophy to preach at times that aid us all, as when one sings :

> " There's a sense you gather, sonny,
>   In the open-air ;
> Shift your burden ere it break you,
>   God will take His share.
> Keep your end up for your own sake,
>   And the rest's His care ! "

Lovers of Scottish verse would greatly enjoy the exquisite verses of Mr. Murray in his little volume of South African poems, entitled, *Hamewith*, which contains a few gems.

Early in the century Australia began to produce her own poets, and many names adorn her list. Some of her poets have felt and interpreted the beauty of the new world scenery, which exerts a spell on the hearts of her lovers, like to that of the homeland in the other hemisphere. Thus we find Dorothea Mackellar writing :

> " Though earth holds many splendours,
>   Whenever I may die,
> I know to what brown country
>   My homing thoughts will fly."

The heart of the people is revealed in many lines, with an honesty and power that touches the deepest feelings within us, as when E. Dysoris of Victoria confesses,

> " We are common men with the faults of most, and a few that our-
>   selves have grown,
> With the good traits, too, of the common herd, and some more that
>   are all our own.
> We have done great deeds in our direst needs, in the horrors of burning
>   drought,
> And at mateship's call have been true through all, to the death with
>   the Furthest Out."

Another of her singers (H. H. Lawson) realises what these days have so abundantly proved that " the better part of a people's life in the storm comes uppermost."

Probably one of the best known stanzas in Australian poetry is that of her steeplechase-riding Member of Parliament, A. L. Gordon,

> " Life is mostly froth and bubble,
>   Two things stand like stone—
> Kindness in another's trouble,
>   Courage in your own."

Several of her writers have caught the deepest meaning of democracy, and voiced it in stirring words. Two brief examples must suffice. The first verse is one by T. Bracken, of New Zealand.

> " O God ! that men would see a little clearer,
>   Or judge less harshly where they cannot see !
> O God ! that men would draw a little nearer
>   To one another—they'd be nearer Thee,
>   And understood."

The second is from H. Lawson, already mentioned,

> " And we will meet amidships on this stout old earthly craft,
>   And there won't be any friction 'twixt the classes fore'n'-aft,
>   We'll be brothers fore'n'-aft,
>   We'll be sisters fore'n'-aft,
>   When the people work together and there ain't no fore'n'-aft."

When we turn to Canada we are met by the verdict of Professor Edgar, that the country possesses " the raw material of literature in abundance, but this material does not seem to germinate." In spite of this opinion the fields of Canada have borne some lovely fruit even in the proverbially difficult gardens to cultivate—those of the Muses.

One of the most noteworthy is Bliss Carman, born in New Brunswick in 1861. His verse is of a very high order, and he has earnest thoughts to convey about the universe in which we live, and our duty to God and man. He is a lover of nature and the wilds, and the spirit of the great spaces has passed into his soul.

> " I am sick of roofs and floors,
>   Naught will heal me but to roam,
> Open me the forest doors,
>   Let the green world take me home."

His prayer is :

> " Make me, O Lord, for beauty,
>   Body, soul and spirit."

He feels that only in giving is there any gain ; and that all we have been able to amass " of beauty or intelligence or power,"

> " It is not mine to hoard,
> It stands there to afford
> Its generous service simply as a flower."

Once more let us hear him utter the challenge of a truly spiritual democracy.

> " What Captain are you for,
> The chartered wrong, or Christ and Liberty ? "

Years ago, as the present writer was sailing up the Saint Lawrence river, he was first introduced to the poems of W. H. Drummond, and he listened, within sight of the shores where the speech is spoken, to those exquisite verses that depict, in so wonderful a way, the life of the French Canadian, in the volume called *The Habitant*. It has been truly said of Drummond that " no poet ever derived his inspiration from simpler themes." One of his French critics notes the truth without vulgarity, the piquancy unmixed with any element of the grotesque that mark his pages. He broke new ground and has no successor of the same sort. The life he pictures for us is that of a people, whom it is a joy to know, whose joys and sorrows become ours through the genius of their interpreter. As they are almost all narrative poems it is next to impossible to give any idea of their beauty and pathos in short quotations, but some slight notion may be conveyed by the following lines, forming the close of *Pelang*—the story the girl tells of how she lost her lover on the night of the wild storm, on which day he had promised to return, but perished in the great forest, and she sits now all alone,

> " Not all alone, for I t'ink I hear
> De voice of ma boy gone long ago ;
> Can hear it above de hurricane,
> An' roar of de rapide down below.
> Yes, yes—Pelang, mouchez garçon !
> I t'ink of you, t'ink of you night an' day,
> Don't mak' no difference seems to me,
> How long de tam you was gone away."

The war has made all England familiar with the poems of R. W. Service, whose *Rhymes of a Red Cross Man* contain his most recent work. He is one who has learned to undertsand and can help us to grasp the secrets of that far Western land, of which he sings in one of his earlier volumes :

> " Have you seen God in His splendours, heard the text that Nature renders ?
> (You'll never hear it in the family pew !)
> The simple things, the true things, the silent men who do things—
> Then listen to the wild,—it's calling you ! "

He styles himself " a gipsy of God," and knows not only the charms of the wilderness, but the burdens of life anywhere.

> " It's dead easy to die,
> It's the keeping on living that's hard."

The war has given him new opportunities, and taught him fresh lessons, and few more touching and helpful verses are to be found than some of those contained in the volume to which reference has already been made. Such poems as *The Fool, Carry On! Only a Boche, Tri-Colour*, and *The Whistle of Sandy McGraw* will live long after the occasion that produced them has passed. He has faith in the future hath this man—

> " Seeing within the worst of War's red rage,
> The gleam, the glory of the Golden Age."

And I think the reason is discoverable in one of his earlier poems, with some lines from which we may fittingly take leave, not only of him, but of all our democratic poets for the present, for the words sum up the greatest of the messages they have for the world :

> " Just Home and Love ! the words are small,
> Four little letters into each,
> And yet you will not find in all
> The wide and gracious range of speech
> Two more so tenderly complete ;
> When angels talk in Heaven above,
> I'm sure they have no words more sweet
> Than Home and Love."

For Colonial Poetry the following volumes of the Canterbury Poets should be consulted, 1s. each. *Australian Ballads, Canadian Poems, New Zealand Verse.* The best larger collections are : *The Oxford Book of Canadian Verse,* W. Campbell ; *The Golden Treasury of Australian Verse,* B. Stevens ; *Treasury of South African Verse,* E. H. Crouch.